INTERSECTION: DAWN

CURRENCY PRESS
The performing arts publisher

A T
⌣
Y P

CURRENT THEATRE SERIES

First published in 2024
by Currency Press Pty Ltd,
Gadigal Land, Suite 310, 46–56 Kippax Street, Surry Hills, NSW 2010, Australia
enquiries@currency.com.au
www.currency.com.au

in association with ATYP

Typeset by Brighton Gray for Currency Press.
Cover design by Bec Herkess and Lillie Bailey for ATYP.

Currency Press acknowledges the Traditional Owners of the Country on which we live and work. We pay our respects to all Aboriginal and Torres Strait Islander Elders, past and present.

A catalogue record for this book is available from the National Library of Australia

Contents

Introduction

Why theatre at all?
... Why do we applaud, and what?
What could it serve? What could it explore?
What are its special properties?

Peter Brook, *The Empty Space*, 1968

Through *Intersection*, ATYP provides not just an empty space, but a process and a place that has meaning—an opportunity for our young writers and actors to share their work, connect with peers from far-off places and, importantly, an audience. They create theatre of our time. *Intersection* serves a wonderful role in creating a space for young writers and actors to play. Here, we find writers on a week-long creative retreat experimenting with ways to bring to the page their imaginings and then, courageously, generously, gifting them to young people across the country to bring them to the stage. Students across Australia in classrooms, halls, loungerooms and backyards directing and acting these plays into being. What a gift for young theatremakers! What a gift for us, their teachers, to witness our students grow and be inspired though the collaborative process towards creative ownership of their performance.

Your experiences, your ideas, your imagination, your creativity matter.

Intersection has been a wonderful opportunity for our students to explore new texts and work together as actor/directors to bring these plays to the stage. Through this process, many students have found their voice and grown in confidence as they journeyed on this collaborative and creative journey. So, if you have a fire in your belly to make theatre, wherever you are in Australia, connect with ATYP and the Intersection Festival ... write, collaborate, create, find an audience and move them. Whether you take a pen, take a seat or take the stage, enjoy the shared creative space that is theatre ... and find your answers to Peter's question, why theatre at all?

May you, the reader, enjoy this collection of plays written for the 2024 ATYP Intersection Festival: Dawn; and remember, *the play is the thing*.

Benjamin Daley, Teacher
Cape Byron Rudolf Steiner School
Always was, always will be, Bundjalung Country

Acknowledgements

ATYP would like to acknowledge that the plays in this publication were created on diverse lands of traditional custodians. ATYP is a company that is based on the traditional lands of the Gadigal people, delivering programs in the lands of our First Nations people across this country, rich with history of storytelling. We pay our respects to Elders past and present.

ATYP acknowledges the support of the Jibb Foundation and the Packer Family Foundation which makes National Studio possible.

These plays were developed thanks to mentorship from George Kemp, Anchuli Felicia King and Lewis Treston, and received further dramaturgy by Jane FitzGerald.

Thank you to all the wonderful writers from ATYP's 2023 National Studio: Jadzea Allen, Emmett Aster, Bella Battersby, Ella Callow-Sussex, Tyler Dias, Taylor Fernandez, Blake Hohenhaus, Aliyah Knight, Tasman McClymont-Griffiths, Callum Mackay, Bronte Locke, Caitlin Monk, Olivia Niethe, Jake Parker, Pip, Makaela Rowe-Fox, Megan Rundle, Naleen Sandhu, Michael van Berkel and el waddingham.

A selection of these plays were first rehearsed and performed by the following schools and performing arts programs in preparation for the Intersection Festival at ATYP's Rebel Theatre, on 6, 7 and 8 August, 2024:

BARKER COLLEGE
Teacher: Pia Midgley

BLUE MOUNTAINS GRAMMAR SCHOOL
Teacher: Cindy Pecovnik

CAPE BYRON RUDOLF STEINER SCHOOL
Teacher: Ben Daley

CAPTIVATE
The performing arts unit of the Catholic Schools Office, Diocese of Parramatta
Teachers: Lucinda Armour and Tim Martin

CERDON COLLEGE
Teacher: Samantha Murphy

EMMAUS COLLEGE, ROCKHAMPTON
Teachers: Nicole Driver and Lynda Dowley

GREENACRE CHRISTIAN COLLEGE
Teacher: DJ Wright

THE HUNTER SCHOOL OF THE PERFORMING ARTS
Teacher: Renee Berger

INNER SYDNEY HIGH SCHOOL
Teachers: Renee Lane and Miriam Rosalki

KATOOMBA HIGH SCHOOL
Teacher: Grace Guild

NEWTOWN HIGH SCHOOL OF THE PERFORMING ARTS
Teacher: Daniel Kavanagh

NORTHERN BEACHES CHRISTIAN SCHOOL
Teacher: Issac Owen

NORTHMEAD CREATIVE AND PERFORMING ARTS HIGH SCHOOL
Teacher: Rowena McCabe

OUR LADY OF MERCY COLLEGE, PARRAMATTA
Teacher: Caroline Rowland

PICTON HIGH SCHOOL
Teacher: Lian Halloran

PENRITH SELECTIVE HIGH SCHOOL
Teacher: Tara Lawson

ST CATHERINE'S SCHOOL, WAVERLEY
Teacher: Amy Robertson

ST IVES HIGH SCHOOL
Teacher: Cate Whittle

ST PETER CLAVER COLLEGE
Teacher: Jason Nash

SHOALHAVEN HIGH SCHOOL
Teacher: Maddie Snape

ATYP encourages anyone producing these works to ensure casting reflects the diversity of young people across Australia today.

Order is Truly a Beautiful Thing

Taylor Fernandez

MARA, *17, female, high school student*

PAUL, *17, male, high school student*

MARA-ACTOR, *a fantasy actor in* MARA*'s mind playing out her thoughts*

PAUL-ACTOR, *a fantasy actor in* MARA*'s (and later* PAUL*'s) mind playing out their thoughts*

An empty room with two chairs. The room is supposed to resemble an empty stage, in the theatrical sense.

—— indicates that a line is cut off by the following line.

/ indicates that a line continues whilst the following line is said.

MARA-ACTOR *and* PAUL-ACTOR *are seated in the chairs, holding scripts.* MARA *stands in front of the two actors. She addresses the audience, in the manner of a conference speaker.*

MARA: Order, I think, is a truly beautiful thing. To give order to rampant obsession, I am staging this performance in my head. I welcome you all here today, at the crack of dawn, to witness my fantasies since they have awakened me from my slumber. My thoughts are gratuitous— perhaps indulgent—and they are best governed by clear direction. In that sense, I am the director. And these are the actors that I am casting within the confines of my mind. [*Gesturing to them appropriately*] You, there, will play me, neurotic Year Twelve student, Mara, and you, over there, will play the mysterious hottie in my English class, Paul.

    MARA *positions herself behind the two actors.*

MARA-ACTOR: Where are we in this scene, sorry?
MARA: At Lydia's seventeenth birthday party, next weekend.
PAUL-ACTOR: Great. So, like this?

PAUL-ACTOR *indicates to his chair.*

MARA: Actually, could I get your chairs a little bit closer?

MARA-ACTOR: Did you have to wake us up at dawn to—

MARA: Cooperate please! Okay, for some context, the situation is this: you've both found a moment in the night to sit together at the party. Paul, you're going to lead with, 'Hey. Did you want any pizza?' and Mara—that's me—is going to say yes. Ready?

MARA-ACTOR *and* PAUL-ACTOR *nod. They both focus themselves in preparation for the performance. They begin.*

PAUL-ACTOR: [*to* MARA-ACTOR] Hey. Did you want any pizza? I can grab you a slice.

MARA-ACTOR: [*to* PAUL-ACTOR] Wow, of course! That is so nice of you, Paul.

MARA: Delivered too obsessively. Come up with something else.

MARA-ACTOR: [*correcting her line*] You can do that.

MARA: Too certain.

MARA-ACTOR: Definitely!

MARA: [*spiralling*] Too eager. Please, for the love of god, do not eat food in front of him. What if he sees cheese stuck between two of your teeth, and then he will think about how disgusting you are, and then think, wow, does she even know how to shower? 'Hello, Medicare? Yeah, it's me, Paul. Can you please check if Mara has private healthcare?'

MARA-ACTOR: [*to* MARA] Fine. What about I just say 'no'?

MARA: 'No'? Sure, try that.

MARA-ACTOR: [*suddenly*] No!

PAUL-ACTOR: Geez, I was just asking.

MARA-ACTOR: [*to* MARA] Um, are we still going or—

MARA: Refine that. From the top, please.

PAUL-ACTOR: Hey. Did you want any pizza? I can grab you a slice.

MARA-ACTOR: No, that's alright. Thanks though.

PAUL-ACTOR: No worries. Enjoying the party?

MARA-ACTOR: Yeah, it's nice to just not be studying and—

MARA: Hold it there! Nobody likes an optimist. Certainly, nobody like Paul *wants* an optimist. Can we try it with a little more cynicism about the world?

PAUL-ACTOR: Enjoying the party?

MARA-ACTOR: Get Dante on the phone and tell him that he was wrong. There are, in fact, ten circles of hell, and we are—

PAUL-ACTOR: In the tenth one right now.

MARA-ACTOR: That's so funny.

MARA: Don't say 'that's so funny'. You'll sound pathetic. God. Just laugh.

> MARA-ACTOR *laughs.*

Laugh louder.

> MARA-ACTOR *laughs louder.*

But like a lady.

> MARA-ACTOR *laughs again, more delicately.*

Perfect. Okay, back to you Paul.

PAUL-ACTOR: Honestly, high school feels like the stage for some disturbing plot, constructed for all these strange actors waiting for their cue.

MARA-ACTOR: Right. Like we are all following a script.

PAUL-ACTOR: Exactly! We've all been assigned our role to play. The funny one cracking jokes in Science. Football guy. Music kid on piano. It's all determined.

MARA-ACTOR: That's their problem, though. None of these people *are* determined.

PAUL-ACTOR: No motivation at all. They are mostly reproductions of the same type of person. My theory is that someone is churning out these mass-produced beings from a factory line.

MARA-ACTOR: That's grim.

PAUL-ACTOR: But you agree, surely?

MARA-ACTOR: I do. Some of Lydia's friends are insufferable.

PAUL-ACTOR: Tell me about it. Do you ever think: I could be seeking something that makes me much happier than having the same boring conversations about maths homework and sleep schedules? We could be enjoying life much more with some pleasurable alternative.

MARA-ACTOR: [*attempting to flirt*] Which pleasure would you like to be seeking?

MARA: Gross. Did I write that?

MARA-ACTOR: [*to* MARA, *pointing at the script*] Yeah, you said—

MARA: Don't undermine me. How about you go with the line … 'if you could be doing something else right now, what would it be?'

MARA-ACTOR: If you could be doing something else right now, what would it be?

PAUL-ACTOR: Watching a movie.

MARA-ACTOR: [*exaggerated*] That's so much fun!

MARA: Bit much.

MARA-ACTOR: [*laidback*] Totally.

PAUL-ACTOR: You know, I place so much value on a movie. I think if some big disaster wiped all of us out, and humanity had to be restored, the only true time capsule would be a good film. Everything will be gone—decayed—and we will think, *how did we ever survive?*

MARA-ACTOR: How *did* we survive?

PAUL-ACTOR: How did we cope?

MARA-ACTOR: We didn't.

PAUL-ACTOR: How did we live? And we will put on some brilliant movie on whatever device is available, and there will be an essence of what we are, *who* we are.

MARA: That's very good. Then you will give him a laugh and smile sweetly.

MARA-ACTOR *obliges.*

Okay, now get him to talk about English with you. Smart boys love that stuff.

MARA-ACTOR: How are you liking *Dorian Gray*?

PAUL-ACTOR: Yeah, I'm enjoying the prose. I've got it in my bag.

PAUL-ACTOR *pulls out a book.*

I found it at Salvos, so it's an ugly edition.

MARA-ACTOR: So you must be getting hotter each day, while the book grows uglier and uglier in the depths of your backpack.

MARA: That wasn't remotely smooth. But we can work with it.

PAUL-ACTOR: You're quite beautiful, you know that?

MARA-ACTOR *and* PAUL-ACTOR *lean in to kiss, abruptly stopped by* MARA*'s interruption.*

MARA: [*to* MARA-ACTOR, *menacingly*] Read the barcode on the back of the book.

MARA-ACTOR: [*dismissively*] Done.

MARA: Read it again. You might have missed something.

MARA-ACTOR: Okay?

MARA: Check it again. Something is not right.

MARA-ACTOR: Uh—

MARA: Go on. Sound it out in your head. Memorise each number.

MARA-ACTOR: [*to* MARA] Paul and I were about to have a moment. You can be quiet now.

MARA: Something bad will happen if you don't. Your dad will die.

MARA-ACTOR: My dad will die?

MARA: Read it!

MARA-ACTOR: [*under breath*] Seven … three … four … three … five … zero …

PAUL-ACTOR: Sorry, what was that?

MARA-ACTOR: Hold on. Nine … three … two …

PAUL-ACTOR: Is everything okay?

MARA-ACTOR: [*suddenly*] I don't want my dad to die!

PAUL-ACTOR: [*confused*] Is he sick?

MARA-ACTOR: No.

> *The moment is over.*

MARA: What the hell? Why did you do that?

MARA-ACTOR: You put it in the script you have been devising for me!

MARA: Well, my sincere apologies, but the audience is bored now. Change it up. Let's get Paul to mention the music.

PAUL-ACTOR: [*to* MARA] Don't you think that we should check on Mara?

MARA: Paul! Focus on your notes! Mention the music!

PAUL-ACTOR: [*to* MARA-ACTOR, *hesitantly*] So, uh, you like the music?

MARA-ACTOR: I think pop music is how they can indoctrinate us mass-produced beings with The Message.

PAUL-ACTOR: What is The Message?

MARA-ACTOR: Conformity … good.

PAUL-ACTOR: Capitalism … also good.

MARA-ACTOR: Freedom … a pathetic illusion.

MARA: Excuse me? What are you on about? You have freedom. You could slap him right now in his smug little face!

MARA-ACTOR: [*to* MARA] Why would I want to do that?

MARA: Slap him! You can just lean forward and hit him!

MARA-ACTOR: Wait. Should I?

MARA: No. Kiss him! Lick his face!

MARA-ACTOR: That's not really possible—

MARA: Yell something profane! Start swearing! Do it!

MARA-ACTOR: [*freaking out*] Um … um …

MARA: Paul, help me out here.

PAUL-ACTOR: Fine. [*To* MARA-ACTOR] What music do you like?

MARA-ACTOR: I'm more into like … Jeff Buckley.

PAUL-ACTOR: Respect. *Grace* is a top-tier album.

MARA: You could hit him!

> MARA-ACTOR *blocks her ears and tries to keep talking to* PAUL-ACTOR.

MARA-ACTOR: [*to* PAUL-ACTOR] You are so cool.

> PAUL-ACTOR *laughs. They look at each other, and* MARA-ACTOR *tucks a strand of hair behind her right ear.*

MARA: That's not symmetrical. I want order. Do it again with the other hand.

> MARA-ACTOR *nervously does the same with hair behind her left ear.*

Repeat it. Do you want the world to end?

> MARA-ACTOR *rapidly keeps tucking strands of her hair behind her ear.*

PAUL-ACTOR: Everything okay, Mara?

> PAUL-ACTOR *grabs* MARA-ACTOR*'s hand, slowing her down. They have another moment, looking at each other, whilst holding hands.*

MARA: [*yelling*] Mara, you idiot! He could contaminate you! Wash your hands! What if he is ill? What if this contact is the reason that you are Case Zero for a new variant of disease? Think about how disgusting you will be! Nobody will want you!

MARA-ACTOR *is visibly distressed.* PAUL *enters and stands next to* MARA; *from that moment on, they only direct and address their respective actor-selves rather than both actors.*

PAUL: [*addressing the audience*] Thank you for joining me here, in the early hours of the morning. There is so much disorder within my mind, you know? I am excited to show you my work-in-development, as I give shape to my anxious thoughts. [*Talking to* PAUL-ACTOR] Can you play me, Paul? You think you can make me not seem too pretentious?

PAUL-ACTOR: I'm trying already.

MARA: [*to* MARA-ACTOR] Can you just continue reading your lines?

The lines overlap each other, as MARA *and* PAUL *talk to the actors in their mind, and* MARA-ACTOR *and* PAUL-ACTOR *attempt to get through to each other.*

MARA-ACTOR: Nobody will want me?

MARA: You're so contaminated now/

MARA-ACTOR: Um, I am feeling overwhelmed/

PAUL: Stop trying to seem cool. You're embarrassing yourself.

MARA: He doesn't even want to talk to you.

PAUL-ACTOR: [*to* MARA-ACTOR] Mara, seriously, is everything okay?

MARA: He doesn't mean that.

MARA-ACTOR: I'm feeling so/

MARA: Repeat the number from the barcode. Check it again. Your dad will die.

PAUL: [*to* PAUL-ACTOR] Why did you say that crap about movies?

MARA: Slap him! Kiss him! Take his germs!

PAUL-ACTOR: Mara!

MARA-ACTOR: How do I/

PAUL: [*mockingly*] '*Grace* is a top-tier album.' Who says that?

MARA: You need more order/

PAUL: There is so much disorder/

MARA-ACTOR: Uh …

PAUL-ACTOR: Um …

MARA *and* PAUL: Do something!

The actors look at each other for a solution.

MARA-ACTOR: Let's improvise.
PAUL-ACTOR: Sounds good.
MARA: Improvise?
PAUL: Sounds … good?

>*Beat.*

PAUL-ACTOR: You okay Mara? Do you need anything?
MARA-ACTOR: I need … order in my life.
PAUL-ACTOR: I get that. I do. Nothing makes sense without structure.
MARA-ACTOR: Order is truly a beautiful thing.
PAUL-ACTOR: But chaos can also be exciting. You know?

>MARA-ACTOR *and* PAUL-ACTOR *stare at each other and smile.*

[*To* PAUL] You can go to sleep now. We can work without your direction.
PAUL: [*to* PAUL-ACTOR] Right. Well, I'm going back to bed. But Mara—
PAUL-ACTOR: [*to* PAUL] will think you're cool, yes. Don't stress about it.
MARA: [*to* MARA-ACTOR] Perhaps I don't need to script next weekend. It will be okay?
MARA-ACTOR: [*to* MARA] Trust me. We can take it from here.

THE END

The Rat Who Fell in Love with The Bird

Blake Hohenhaus

RAT, *14 to 17 years old. Any gender.*

BIRD, *14 to 17 years old. Any gender.*

— at the end of a line indicates the point where a character is interrupted.

... indicates a character trailing off / thinking.

/ indicates the point in a line where the next line begins, overlapping.

RAT *speaks quickly, nervously.* BIRD *takes their time, well-paced. The actors are encouraged to play with the script's openness towards how it's played in the physical space, and to explore the difference between conversation, monologues and 'texting-speak'.*

Early in the play, RAT *refers to 'swimmers' and 'togs'. The word 'swimmers' should be swapped out for the local colloquialism for swimwear, unless the local colloquialism is 'togs', in which case the words should simply swap.*

The personal pronouns for both RAT *and* BIRD *in this script are written as he/him/his and is inherently a queer love story. However, and most importantly, anyone of any gender can play either of the characters. The personal pronouns should be changed to represent accurately the gender of the players. Love is universal and the players should feel inspired to explore how* RAT *and* BIRD *feel and show that love, and what it means within their context, regardless of gender.*

Also important: Nobody in this play ever holds a phone or mimes holding a phone.

RAT *is standing behind the counter at a shop. The only thing that suggests he might be a Rat is the words that he says. He turns to the audience.*

RAT: Consider the Rat.

Nocturnal. Solitary. Lover of cheese. We Rats *really* like cheese.

[*Gesturing towards themselves*] This Rat even works in a cheese shop. I earn fifteen-sixty an hour two times a week by selling Bries and Goudas to smiley sixty-year-olds.

We Rats *thrive* in the depths of the night. Nighttime is our time. I scamper around the house at two a.m. avoiding the pressures of the next day. But that means I'm now doing the Thursday night shift after five hours' sleep and a full day of school … It's hard being a Rat.

A person is born a Rat, and no matter how hard they try, they can't get to bed early enough or wake up in time for *anything*. That talent is reserved for the *Bird*. For the Bird, *daytime* is their domain. They wake early with confidence, vitality and joy. Rats and Birds are incompatible: polar opposites.

My little conundrum though is that *this* Rat is in love with a Bird.

BIRD *appears on stage.*

BIRD: Hi.

RAT: [*to the audience, surprised*] This bird.

[*To* BIRD] Hi.

BIRD: I didn't know you worked here.

RAT: [*bewildered*] Neither did—Yeah. I do. How can I help … you?

BIRD: I was just hoping to get some cheese for my mum.

RAT: [*still bewildered*] Right …

BIRD: Because it's Mother's Day on Sunday and this is a cheese shop.

RAT: Uh huh.

BIRD: Are you okay?

RAT: [*returning to earth*] Yes!

RAT *walks out from behind the counter.*

So! We have some lovely / gift boxes

BIRD: You're *the Rat*, right?

RAT: [*to the audience*] He didn't call me that. But it's what I heard.

Yeah … That's me.

BIRD: Cool.

> *Beat. They look at each other.* RAT *loses himself for a moment and then remembers the cheese at hand.*

RAT: [*quickly*] Ah so we have the *Le Fromage* Gift Set which is actually really popular 'cause it comes with a collectable / teacup
BIRD: We have *History* together, right?

> *Beat.* RAT *gulps.*

RAT: [*to the audience, quickly*] We do have history, but does he mean Grade Eight: when we held the Kenny House banner together at the swimming carnival? Or Grade Nine camp: when he told me it was 'cute' that I called swimmers *togs*? Or all the times he's ever looked at me from where his group sits at lunch??

> [*To* BIRD, *playing it cool*] Yeah, we totally do.

BIRD: Thought so! Sir's such a noodle, hey.
RAT: Sir?

> *Beat.*

Oh! Yeah *totally*. History *class*!
BIRD: [*smiling*] … Yeah.

> *Beat.*

RAT: [*quickly*] Okay-so-this-one's-got-a-teacup-which-is-pretty-cool, an—
BIRD: Do you usually work Thursday nights?
RAT: Uh … most Thursday nights; I finish at nine-thirty.
BIRD: Damn! That's so late!
RAT: [*to the audience, rolling his eyes*] Pfff. Birds.

> [*Covering*] *SO* late … yeah.

BIRD: [*vivaciously*] Well, I've got training tomorrow morning, park-run Saturday morning, then soccer Saturday arvo so that's why *I'm* here tonight!
RAT: Oh yeah. Cool.
BIRD: Do you run?

> RAT *shakes his head.*

You should! It feels like you're *flying* when you really get into it. If you wanted, I could—

RAT: [*to the audience*] Rats don't *fly*, they scamper.

    [*Back to the gift-pack*] Yeah cool maybe well … this one is really pretty I'm guessing your mum might / like it …

BIRD: Yep, I'll get that one. Thanks.

    A shift. RAT *turns to the audience.*

RAT: So that was the day the Rat sold a teacup to the Bird. When I was done gift-wrapping the *Le Fromage* he said

BIRD: I'll see you in History.

RAT: and I said 'Enjoy your flight' and he said

BIRD: What?

RAT: and I said 'oh, sorry, I meant run … '

    'Lol.'

    and he left.

    BIRD *leaves.*

[*To the audience*] On Monday, I'm in History class.

    BIRD *re-enters with two chairs. One for* RAT, *one for* BIRD.

The Bird is sitting two rows behind me, which he always does, and usually that's fine, but *now* I know he knows that I know he knows who I am and that I'm in his class and that I sit two rows in front of him.

    BIRD *sticks his hand up.*

BIRD: Hey sir! Do you reckon we actually landed on the moon?

    RAT *sighs.*

RAT: This lesson is about the Roman Empire.

BIRD: Yeah 'cause I saw a thing that said that a movie director faked it to help the US government win the World War One or something …

RAT: Some people say that Birds have smaller brains than Rats. But I think he just says these things to make his friends laugh.

BIRD: Yeah like Quentin Tarantino, I think …

RAT: And the friends *do* laugh. It's the kind of Big Group Laugh that sometimes sounds like it could be directed at you if you're not careful … Good thing Rats are careful.

BIRD: I dunno sir, it just seems a bit sus.

RAT: Birds can be loved for their other qualities though!

    Like their song.

BIRD *laughs loudly.*

The way they … preen themselves.

BIRD *tussles his hair and/or fixes his shirt.*

The way they keep a watchful eye over the rest of the …

RAT *searches for the right description.*

Animal … kingdom …

BIRD *looks over at the 'desk' next to him and speaks to another—invisible—'student'.*

BIRD: [*earnestly*] Hey, you got a B-minus on the exam? Good work dude, that's an improvement, right?

RAT: I *do* love the Bird but sometimes I worry if really, I just want to *be* the Bird; someone everyone loves. A representative of the flow of life itself.

Class is over. BIRD *gets out of his seat.*

But I am forever a Rat …

BIRD: Hey Rat!

RAT *jumps.*

RAT: Hi.

BIRD: Just wanted to say, like … thanks for the gift box. Mum really liked it.

RAT: Oh! No worries. Thought she would.

BIRD: She said, 'why'd you pick this one' and I said 'this person in my class named Rat' picked it out for me.

RAT: She didn't think it was a … cheesy gift?

BIRD: Nah of course not …

Beat. RAT *waits, gestures.*

Oh. Ha! You're funny, Rat. See ya later maybe?

BIRD *leaves.* RAT *stands up. The chairs go.*

RAT: I go home. Then, I get a text.

BIRD *enters, side stage.*

BIRD: HEY all caps. rat lower-case. i've been trying to figure out how to say this for a while but i think ur real cool and if u wanna meet me at the top of the Mountain tomorrow morn before sunrise, maybe i can talk to u more about it and we can watch the sun come up or somethin. i hope u know what i mean and feel the same way lmao. if not that's all good i just hope you can be cool about it. maybe see u there?

RAT: Holy shi—

hey! i definitely feel the same. would love to meet u at the Mountain tomorrow

BIRD: wow okay cool! sunrise is at six so i'll meet u at the top at five-thirty?

RAT: yeah defs. smiley face

Beat.

BIRD: smiley face. xx

BIRD *exits, side stage.*

RAT: [*to the audience*] … x x.

Oh. My god.

Six a.m. is only three hours after the usual three a.m. Rat bedtime. But, to love a Bird, a Rat must be willing to make sacrifices. I once overheard Bird talking about *how* he gets up so early. It was something about

BIRD *crosses stage with his next two lines, talking to invisible friends.*

BIRD: the mindset.

RAT: and

BIRD: the will to get up and get that *bread.*

Beat.

RAT: I wanted that bread.

RAT *takes a deep breath.*

So here I am at eleven p.m., the earliest bedtime in years, channelling the *mindset*, a cacophony of cascading alarms ready to awaken me, in … the …

The RAT gestures towards 'going to sleep' but halfway through the gesture he is interrupted suddenly by the sound of the 'Emergency' iPhone alarm overlapping on itself.

[*Wearily*] Morning— [*With clarity*] Oh GOD!

This next section is delivered quickly.

Rats aren't good at waking up. I slept through *ten* alarms.
I get up and throw some clothes on.
I jog down the street.
I start climbing the Mountain.
It's tricky to see where I'm going in the twilight.
I'm scampering as fast as I can.
My feet slip on rocks.
The sky is getting brighter, the sun is coming.
I feel like I'll never make it.
But then …
I reach the top.

RAT *looks around with an extraordinary sense of hope. A deep breath.*

And there is nobody. Nothing. No Bird.

Beat. A realisation.

Oh. He's tricked me.
I can feel his talons digging into my skin. I can hear him and his friends laughing at me. [*Angry, disappointed*] A Rat should know better than to love a Bird. We belong in the night, and I should have *stayed* there.

Beat. We hear the murmuring caws of cockatoos beginning to wake. Over the remainder of this scene, the sun rises.

But then I see it. The sun. Rising above the horizon right before my eyes. Looking out across the valley, basking in the fresh light, I see now all the majesty that Rats cannot know. I see how it is to wake with the world. I *understand* it.

I am capable of *unknowable evolution*. Rats *can* change. Because *look* at me here at the top of this mountain! With wings broad and beautiful! I don't *need* the Bird, because here *I* am, no longer a Rat. Here *I* am, undeniably into a Bird transformed!

RAT *closes his eyes, stretching out his arms, basking in the glory of transformation and this newfound understanding. Then suddenly—*

BIRD *appears from behind the* RAT, *catching his breath.*

BIRD: Oh … my god. I'm … so sorry. My alarm didn't wake me up, I *really* gotta work on getting to bed earlier …

RAT *looks at* BIRD, *stunned.* BIRD *notices the look on his face.*

Did you think I wasn't coming?

RAT: Kind of, yeah …

BIRD: Oh I'm so *so* sorry.

RAT: That's okay, Charlie.

[*Gently, to the audience*] That's Bird's name.

BIRD: I'm really glad you're here, Jesse.

RAT: [*gently, to the audience*] And that's mine.

BIRD *walks over to* RAT *and gently takes his hand.* RAT *smiles. They look towards dawn.*

THE END

Four Legs Good

Aliyah Knight

MAX, *16, female/female-presenting.* ZOYA*'s best friend. Drama kid.*

ZOYA, *17, female/female-presenting.* MAX*'s best friend.* Not *a drama kid.*

At certain points our characters acknowledge one another during moments of direct address. Whilst MAX *and* ZOYA *cannot literally hear one another's thoughts, they wish they could. Play with that!*

The aftermath of the school play wrap party. We assume that there are bodies asleep throughout the house. MAX *and* ZOYA *are still in their homemade* Animal Farm *costumes.* MAX *stands on one side of the room, buzzing with energy but seemingly uncomfortable with her surroundings.* ZOYA *lies on a couch on the other side of the room, feigning sleep. They're at the end of Year Eleven and on the edge of the rest of their lives.*

ZOYA: [*to audience*] Alright, let's get this over with. I'm aware of how ridiculous I look. I know that there aren't any kangaroos in *Animal Farm*. I know that it doesn't make any narrative sense and that it 'threatens the integrity of the play' or whatever. I *know* that. I also know that Emma McPherson telling everyone to stay in costume for the entire afterparty *and* overnight to 'say goodbye to the character' is a full-blown crime against humanity. I should've just stuck with debate. I only auditioned in the first place because / I know

MAX: [*to audience*] I know what you're thinking. What was that up the back? I should've been Napoleon? Stop, that's so awkward! You can't say that! You're right though: I should have been Napoleon. The only reason that I wasn't is because I'm a Year Eleven and that 'wouldn't have been fair' to the Year Twelves, but like … *screw* that. Isn't art supposed to *challenge* people? I was honestly going to quit in protest, but I really wanted to see Zoya as a kangaroo up close.

ZOYA: [*to audience*] Max really cares about this theatre business. And I really care about Max. Even though I don't fully get why she cared so much about what pig she got cast as. I mean … they're pigs. They're *pigs*.

MAX *turns back to* ZOYA, *confused.*

MAX: Huh? Did you say something? / Zoya?

MAX *crosses over to* ZOYA, *who curls up again and begins to fake-snore.*

MAX *prods* ZOYA, *who—trying to avoid* MAX*—doesn't give in.* MAX *then returns to the other side of the room.*

[*To audience*] Weird. Anyway … it was doomed from the start. Right? Like, that's what you're all thinking. I should've just quit the stupid play as soon as they decided to blow out the candle of my creative potential. You're all thinking that, and I agree. That way, I wouldn't have had to be a part of the apocalyptic level disaster that was watching Zoya trying to flirt with Emma McPhearson all throughout the party last night. Napoleon. My *nemesis*. Zoya's not supposed to like people. Or want people. Or feel any emotion towards anybody except loving her parents or finding me really funny or being obsessed enough with Dua Lipa that she'll finally consider my thoroughly researched plan for how we can both end up as her backup dancers. What if Emma brainwashes her into only listening to orchestral jazz and musical theatre and then I have to take Grandma Joan with me to her next concert? Zoya's not supposed to like *girls*—Wait, delete. That sounded bad. I'm an ally!

ZOYA: [*to audience*] I think this is the most pathetic I've ever felt, and I currently hold the school record for most own-goals scored in a single soccer game. I've *been* pathetic. It's just … I'm in Cameron Walker's living room wearing a kangaroo costume. I smell like a mix of lemon fat lamb and Emma's vomit. And I watched Max make out with *Cameron Walker* last night. *All* night.

I should be used to it by now. Max likes a guy, they hook up, end scene. Or, end scene for her, at least. They all stay totally in love with her, but she never really seems to notice, or care, which would be soooooo girlboss if I wasn't so …

ZOYA *looks to the audience as though to say: don't make me say it.*

MAX: [*to audience*] Zoya's not supposed to like Emma. She's just … never looked at anybody like that before! Not even *me*, and I got voted joint second hottest Year Eleven girl! The only reason I didn't win was because one of the Year Twelves got mad that I didn't wanna do stuff with him in character last term. Sure, Lady Macbeth's hot, but it's an emotionally demanding role! And he definitely doesn't understand her complexity! Emma didn't get voted as anything, but Zoya kept on staring at her like she wanted to peel her stupid little skin off her little body and then eat her or something, like a deranged *loser*.

ZOYA: [*to audience*] You know. It's the whole cliche, isn't it?
    She doesn't know, of course.

MAX *turns towards* ZOYA, *exasperated.*

MAX: [*to audience*] Am I actually going insane? I swear she just said something.
    [*To* ZOYA] Zoya?

ZOYA: [*to audience*] I'll bite the bullet.

ZOYA *sits up properly; she can't run away forever.*

Morning.

MAX: Morning, sunshine. Good night?

ZOYA: Was for you.

MAX: Well, no, not really. I hardly got to talk to you.

ZOYA: Your mouth was otherwise engaged.

MAX: Most guys kiss like fishes, did you know that? You're lucky, I've heard girls are much better. I'm sure you'll find out soon enough, hey?

ZOYA: What does that mean?

MAX: Well, just … Emma McPhearson.

ZOYA: What about Emma?

MAX: Well. She's gay. You're gay.

ZOYA: Thank you, Max! How could I have missed it? Would you like to plan the wedding or officiate it?

MAX: I … I thought you liked her? What about last night? And chess club!

ZOYA *laughs in frustration, then collapses onto the sofa.*

ZOYA: I don't like Emma, I just actually like chess! She spent half the night complaining that I wasn't committed enough to the given circumstances of being a kangaroo and the other half throwing up on me.

MAX: Zoya, you didn't commit enough. You hopped like, twice in the whole thing.

ZOYA: I pulled a muscle!

MAX: You *do* like somebody though! Cameron said he saw you curled up on the dog bed watching TikTok edits of *Portrait of a Lady / on Fire*.

ZOYA: Well if *Cameron Walker* says so!

MAX: [*confused*] You don't have to say his full name.

ZOYA: I want to say his full name. To emphasise. How much I *hate* him.

MAX: And why do you hate him?

ZOYA: Because his house is ugly.

MAX *looks at* ZOYA *expectantly.*

And his pool is freezing! And … he was a really bad stage manager and an even *worse* Macbeth. You know, one time I offered him an M&M and he put his entire hand in and started rummaging instead of just taking one. Because … he spied on me last night during my mindfulness break! Because he can somehow get any girl he wants even though his Robert de Niro impression is nowhere near as good as mine. Because he *kissed you*!

That hangs in the air for a second.

MAX: Oh … kay. Um. Well, your Robert de Niro impression is pretty good.

ZOYA: [*instinctively, in a Robert de Niro accent*] 'It's a fish eat fish world'.
     [*Realising* MAX *has veered her off topic*] No! Stop it! UGH!
     [*To audience*] I didn't mean to tell her like that. I can't believe I'm *that* lesbian. Setting back the community another fifty million years by being in love with my best friend. I want to say it's kind of worth it, but that'd just be sad, given that she's currently in the process of rejecting me. Speaking of, can she hurry up with it? Hit me baby one more time.

MAX: [*to audience*] I totally didn't mean to respond like that. She's just wearing that ridiculous kangaroo costume, and it reminds me of the time that I got almost-attacked by a kangaroo at the lake and everybody laughed at me because I started crying, like, a lot. But Zoya just stroked my hair and I felt super weird and like I really wanted to jump on a trampoline for the rest of the day. Almost like I wanted to … oh. Oh.

[*To* ZOYA] Robert de Niro was kinda hot in the nineties.

ZOYA: What?

MAX: What? You're right. Irrelevant. Well, you're definitely not mad at Cameron because you wanted to kiss *him*.

ZOYA: No. That would be pretty contradictory. I am gay.

MAX: So … that means you wanted to kiss me.

A long beat.

You wanted to kiss *me*.

ZOYA: Yep. Heard you the first time, Max.

MAX: Well? Did you?

A moment of silence tells us what we need to know.

[*Softly*] Oh. I wish I'd known. I told you, they all kiss like fishes.

ZOYA: I might kiss like a fish. One of those weird jawless ones. I haven't had a heap of practice.

MAX: But you're my favorite person. I never even thought … If I'd known …

ZOYA *looks to* MAX *curiously, trying not to get her hopes up.*
MAX *becomes exceedingly interested in her shoelaces.*

ZOYA: Oh. Well, um. Kangaroos can't kiss … pigs.

MAX *laughs—it's the good kind of deflating, letting all of the air out of her system—then walks over to* ZOYA, *dropping her pig ears to the floor.* ZOYA *does the same with her kangaroo ears.*

MAX: Good thing you're not a Kangaroo then. Even though it suits you.

ZOYA: No, you can be honest. I didn't find the authenticity of being a kangaroo.

MAX: You really didn't. Good thing I like you anyway.

ZOYA: Yeah. Me too.

MAX *reaches out to hold* ZOYA*'s hand.* ZOYA *accepts. They move forward and look out.*

MAX: Sun's out. D'you wanna go on Cameron's trampoline? I've been thinking about it all morning.

ZOYA *looks at her hands, then at* MAX. *She grins.*

ZOYA: I can do a somersault.

Hand in hand, they leave the room.

THE END

The Turtleneck

Bronte Locke

LAURA, *15 years old. Twin of Paulie. The younger twin by six minutes.*

PAULIE, *15 years old. Twin of Laura. The older twin by six minutes.*

Laura has been written as she/her and Paulie as he/him, but these pronouns and names can change to reflect the pronouns of the performers.

Regarding staging, all you need is an order of service, something to put it on, a turtleneck and a sandwich. All other props and actions can be mimed.

A slow Tuesday afternoon. The bathroom of a suburban bowls club. The bathroom is not a stall situation, rather, a room with a toilet. An old sink with old taps, a bowl of dust-covered seashell-shaped soaps (decorative) and a cake of greying and cracked Imperial Leather soap (functional). Next to the basin lies an order of service. There's a sort of magical, liminal feeling to this place. Just offstage, a wake is well underway.

We hear a toilet flush, then lights up. LAURA *stands next to the toilet (finger on the button). She's wearing a thick lavender turtleneck. You can see she is physically affected by the constriction and itchiness of the garment.*

LAURA *speaks directly to the audience, there's a confessional element to it.*

LAURA: Mum bought this jumper for me, said it was age appropriate.
    'Fifteen-year-olds don't wear black to a funeral, they don't know death like that.

    There's something ominous to this.

Yet.'

So, she bought me this lavender turtleneck, which is HOT, and really itchy around here—

LAURA *points to the neck.*

And before, when I was handing out date loaf, an old lady turned to me and said:
'Sweetheart, your jumper's on back to front.'
And I said:
'Turtlenecks don't have a back or a front, they're a circle!'

Beat.

She was right.
So I'm in the loo fixing it.
First I had a wee ('cause I drank a lot of cordial), *now* I'll fix it.

She moves to fix her jumper, but something in her screams 'NO'.

Gotta wash my hands!

LAURA *approaches the sink. Her eyes find the order of service and she stops dead in her tracks. The paper is luminous in this light, ethereal, ghost-like.*

But someone's left an order of service next to the sink.
It's got a photo of my all-time favourite lady on the front.
It's sparkling in the sunlight, thanks to the pearlescent paper upsold by Deborah (from White Lady Funerals).
I've made it this far without looking at it. Really, I've managed to avoid most of the day.
I turned my order of service into a chatterbox!
But even after all the folding and bending, I could still make out all the photos Mum picked the day after. So I made it into a paper plane and flew it into the rose garden!
I'm trying to pack away all these yucky emotions and open that box in my forties.
Not today, feelings!

A loud KNOCK interrupts her monologuing, and LAURA*'s caught out.*

The lighting shifts to something drab and pedestrian (we'll call this duologue lighting).

Oops.

PAULIE, LAURA's *twin brother, enters.*

He's wearing a lavender button-down and eating an egg and lettuce sandwich.

There's an air of casual charm to him. He knocks on the door.

PAULIE: Hello? Anyone in there?

PAULIE *knocks harder this time, yelling:*

HELLO?

PAULIE *goes to open the door,* LAURA *stops him.*

LAURA: Occupied.

PAULIE: Laura?

LAURA: Yeah?

PAULIE: It's Paulie!

LAURA: I know, Paulie.

PAULIE: I thought you might've been one of Nan's friends.
Saw a few of them take out their hearing aids during Mum's eulogy.

LAURA: Lucky.

PAULIE: I've been doing the rounds, and I think most of them forgot to put 'em back in. Lots of yelling …
'No, PAULIE, I'm her grandson. GRANDSON!
Yeah, I do have very feminine facial features—
You can't say that anymore, Doreen!'

LAURA *isn't really listening; she's looking at the order of service on the edge of the sink.*

You done?

LAURA: No.

PAULIE: Reckon you'll be long? Doreen brought egg and lettuce sandwiches and I ate six.
And this is the only bathroom.

LAURA: I'll be a while.

PAULIE: Ahhhhhh, you ate some of her sandwiches too. Take your time.

LAURA: Thanks.

PAULIE: No wozzas. See ya.

PAULIE *exits, finishing the sandwich.*

We're back to the magic monologue lighting.

LAURA *picks up the order of service but doesn't look at it.*

LAURA: Laura, stop. Tape up the box—

LAURA *can't help herself; she reads it.*

A Celebration of the Life of Dawn Elliot-Fitzpatrick.
Born: May twentieth, nineteen-forty-one.
Died: January eighteenth, twenty-twenty-four.
Survived by her loving daughter Jenny, blah blah blah blah,
A list of people I only see at Christmas, blah blah blah blah,
A list of people I've never *met*: her beautician, Belinda (wow) …
And her two beautiful grandchildren: Paulie and Lauren.

She pauses, perplexed.

Lauren?! My name's not Lauren.

A profoundly joyful realisation.

It's Laura!
I knew something about today felt *off*!
It wasn't the UE Boom disconnecting during the opening song.
It wasn't the memorial portrait up front, which was facetuned, and superimposed onto a rising sun.
It wasn't watching the coffin slip away on an afterlife version of a supermarket slide-y thing. That thing you put your groceries on.
And after, you put a rectangular block which lets the person behind you know you've got all your stuff on there.
Did they put one of those behind the coffin? To let the crematorium checkout chick know there's no life left. No laughing left. No taking me to Westfield, where we'd sit and drink mochas without the coffee and look at orthopaedic sandals for her funny feet.
Just body and bones and her favourite jumper that smelt like talcum powder.

A horrific realisation.

But where does she go after?! Do they scan her? Is it a click-and-collect? Does she go into a reusable bag?

MUM ALWAYS FORGETS THEM!

As PAULIE *runs in, the lighting shifts back to the duologue state.*
He brings a new and very real sense of urgency.

PAULIE: Laura? Hurry up! I have to poo!

PAULIE *doubles over in a gas-trapped pain.*

LAURA: I'm washing my hands.

PAULIE: There's hand sanitiser in the kitchen—

LAURA: No. Go across the road to the park, there'll be a toilet there.

PAULIE: I can't make it that far, it *has* to be in there.

Or whatever cake tin I can find in the kitchen.

LAURA: Make sure it's a big one.

PAULIE: LAURAAAAAAAHHHHHH!

Let me in! PLEASE!

PAULIE *waits for* LAURA *to open the door.*

AHHHHH!!!!!!!!

PAULIE *runs offstage.*

LAURA *waits for a moment, making sure he's left, then the*
lighting shifts back to the monologue state. Like a detective
piecing together the final bits of a mystery, she continues.

LAURA: But since there's no reusable bags. And no crematorium
checkout chick,

Nan's not dead!

And 'cause Nan's not dead, Mum didn't spend three hours with
Deborah (from White Lady Funerals) arguing about what paper to
use for the order of service.

And Deborah didn't write a list of the most important people in
Nan's life and put some random named Lauren at the bottom.

LAURA *becomes more and more frantic.*

And Mum didn't stand in the driveway this morning and scream:
'Deborah and I agreed the turtleneck fits the sunrise aesthetic.
I'm not LEAVING TILL YOU PUT IT ON! Stop it.
Stop. Crying. You'll ruin your make-up.'

LAURA *is spent.*

Nan would've let me cry off my mascara. And wear a black dress 'cause I'm sad.

And squeezed my hand at the bit in the eulogy where Mum pronounced homage like hummus.

Yeah. Nan's not dead.

LAURA *looks at the order of service like someone looks at a winning Lotto ticket.*

And some girl called Lauren is about to get some *very* upsetting news!

PAULIE *re-enters.*

He KNOCKS, it's softer this time. As he speaks the colour slowly seeps out of the space until all that's left is the bathroom of a suburban bowls club (duologue lighting).

PAULIE: Laura? You right? You've been in there for *ages*.

LAURA: I'm fine.

PAULIE: I couldn't find any good cake tins.

And Mum wants you to hand out the date loaf, she told me I was too rough with the napkins.

Then she made me do the tea, but I kept spilling it into the saucers.

So, she screamed and threw a cup at Aunty Ruth's head, then curled into a ball and started crying so hard she gagged.

LAURA: Is Mum alright?

PAULIE: Nah. But, she's stopped gagging. Still on the floor, though.

Uncle Rod is trying to get the projector working, he wants to start karaoke.

But I've hidden the HDMI cable.

Beat.

Out of respect.

LAURA: Okay.

PAULIE: Maybe it's time to come out of the toilet.

This is the only one.

And I *really* have to go.

Offstage, a karaoke version of 'Hotel California' by the Eagles (or similar seventies-feeling song) starts to play.

LAURA: I don't think you hid it well enough.

PAULIE: Come out Laura.

Help me, please.

LAURA: I can't.

My turtleneck's the wrong way round.

PAULIE: Well, put it the right way round. Then you can help me get Mum off the floor.

LAURA: And help her pass out date loaf.

PAULIE: Yeah.

LAURA: And explain to Nan's lawn bowls team that my name's Laura, not Lauren.

PAULIE: I can help you with that.

After I deal with my thing.

LAURA: And stand around Nan's friends and talk about all the funny things she said.

And walk the oldies to the cars and fold up their wheely walkers and wave them off.

And then I can wash up dirty cups and saucers and dry them with old tea towels.

And do all that little stuff that helps me get that Nan's really Gone.

LAURA *lets herself really feel this feeling.*

It's the first real one in this very long day.

PAULIE: Come out of the bathroom, Laura.

Please.

LAURA *goes to open the door.*

Then, her entire body stiffens.

She places the order of service back on the edge of the sink.

LAURA: Not yet.

Blackout.

THE END

Pest

Callum Mackay

ANNELISE ASHLEY, *15*.

Setting: Principal Nelson's office.

Time: 1:15 p.m.

ANNELISE *sits on a chair wearing a school uniform and holding a hockey stick.*

ANNELISE: Before I explain, Principal Nelson, I want to make one thing crystal clear:

I believe we are all worthy of the love of a cockroach.

Now, don't get me wrong: I'm well aware that what I did today could be perceived as … 'morally unsound'. But I will not find myself questioning my moral existence as *you* should, Mr Nelson. In fact, I've realised that I have maybe, possibly … discovered it.

Beat.

Let's take a step back, shall we?

Five fifty-five a.m.: this morning—Monday (my favourite day of the week).

I rise at dawn, beginning with one-point-five kilometres of freestyle plus a light two-hundred-metre breaststroke to cool down before a long shower and a brief ten minute read of the financial section of *The Age*.

I've scheduled a meeting with you this morning, Principal Nelson: eight thirty to eight fifty a.m. A meeting that has been in your Google Calendar since Friday:

'MEETING WITH ANNELISE ASHLEY.

TOPIC: PETITION TO STOP RYAN MORBY'S PUBLIC EXTERMINATION OF THE BROWN BANDED COCKROACH.

IMPORTANCE: EXTREME.'

I endeavour to always arrive early. Sue me. But I understand, Mr Nelson, that maybe you don't possess such an impressive talent. Two, three, five minutes—that is a length of time I am willing to wait. But FIFTEEN MINUTES I stand outside your office before I receive your less than adequate email:

[*As Mr Nelson*] '*Dear Annelise,*

I'm sorry for my absence this morning. I had a last-minute appointment.

I've read your petition and have extreme concerns. There is much to discuss with you after lunch.

Thank you kindly,

Principal Nelson.'

'Sorry', 'concern', 'extreme', 'discuss' ... 'kindly'?

She takes a deep inhale of breath.

THIS SCHOOL HAS STOOD WITNESS TO COCKROACH MASS MURDER. ALL YOU NEED TO DO IS SIGN MY FREAKIN' PETITION BEFORE RYAN DESTROYS AGAIN AND—

... in through the nostrils, out through the mouth ... *a sip of tea* ... in through the nostrils, out through the mouth ... *lavender oil* ... in through the nostrils, out through the mouth ... RAGE!

Look, I don't have time to have a full mental breakdown, dear Principal. The day has yet to begin. Besides, I have Chapel choir in twelve minutes and they simply won't survive without my soprano.

Eight forty-eight a.m.: I send a curt but respectful email back to you requesting your signature by the start of lunch. Pressing play on my choir scales, I am power walking to the assembly hall, continuing my all-but-ordinary Monday.

Oh, and I'm right! Choir does need me. Sophia is sick and Jake Kelly has a callback for the touring production of *The Boy from Oz* featuring Anthony Callea ... you didn't hear that from me.

That's when he arrives: Ryan Morby and his braindead gang of jocks sneering through my solo as Ryan experiments whether or not he can fit his left testicle into the top of a can of Red Bull.

Nine thirty a.m.: Advanced English—tediously predictable.

Mrs Stephens is clearly far more preoccupied with whatever 'spiritual journey' her psychiatrist is taking her on rather than taking in Benjamin Marcus' startling inquiry of:

[*As Benjamin*] 'Oi, Miss—is Shakespeare dead?'

Ten fifteen a.m.: PE—beep test in the gym.

Kat Redding and I destroy our competition with a respectable eleven-point-five result and as the rest of the class go change, she tells me my solo of 'Ave Maria' was 'divine'. She's a Jesus girl but she did tell me once that she feels a little peculiar whenever we hug ...

Eleven a.m. I'm truly starting to worry about you, Principal Nelson. I once had immense respect for you but an unexplained absence midway through a school day is incredibly disappointing. I decide to visit your receptionist, Carol, to enquire as to your whereabouts. I'd read on a mother's group text chain I'd infiltrated that Carol will soon be celebrating her eighty-first birthday. So, in exchange for information, I offer her a pre-heated blueberry muffin but the witch is onto me:

[*As Carol*] 'I do not accept bribes, Annelise.'

I snatch the muffin off of Carol's desk and wish her an unhappy birthday. This world is harsh, Principal Nelson ... and this girl is fresh outta allies.

Eleven thirty a.m.: Algebra with Mr Jackson.

Whilst I attempt to block out Sadie Smith's pathetic crack at using algebraic puns as a flirtation tactic, I can't help but let my mind wander to your abrasive email this morning:

[*As Mr Nelson*] '*Extreme concerns ...*'

Turning to the last page of my exercise book, I construct a table, rearranging the email, circling words to reveal a coded truth. But before I can come to any conclusion, out of the corner of my eye I spot Ryan outside sitting in the gutter with a bunsen burner:

'RYAN MORBY IS SETTING COCKROACHES ALIGHT IN THE QUADRANGLE!'

[*As Mr Jackson*] 'It's Ryan's free period, Annelise. He can do whatever he wants.'

'BUT, MR. JACKSON, SIR. IT'S—'

[*As Mr Jackson*] 'Shouldn't you be working, Annelise?'

I snap my least-favourite Smiggle pencil and steal Sadie's purple highlighter. Writing in big block letters, I slam my exercise book against the window:

'BURN IN HELL, BOOF HEAD.'

Ryan looks up, takes a minute to sound out the words and gives me the middle finger.

The bell rings. I sprint to the quadrangle—*don't be dead ... please don't die ...*

SURVIVE YOU EIGHT-LEGGED-BEAUTIFUL-SON-OF-A—

But I'm too late. The pyromaniac has escaped.

I sink to my knees, and blow on the sizzling cockroach in my palm, my tears cool the flames:

[*Singing*] 'Ave Maria ... '

I bury the cockroach in the memorial garden next to the carpark, as the second bell rings:

Twelve fifteen p.m.: Ancient History and soon, Ryan Morby will be too.

I kiss the grave, take a deep breath and stand to face my destiny but the number plate of a blue Toyota Camry catches my curiosity: *GREG Five-Oh-Three-Three.*

Finally ... you'd arrived.

I sprint around the gardens, through the halls, past a napping Carol: 'Sir, Mr Nelson—please, Ryan Morby has done it again! HE HAS TO BE STOPPED!'

[*As Mr Nelson*] 'I cannot sign your petition, Annelise.'

You read from the bound copy of the petition I'd slipped into your pigeon hole earlier:

[*As Mr Nelson*] '"*Section Four: In the event of a brutal cockroach slaying, Annelise Ashley will hold primary power and can delegate punishment as she so may wish.*" I cannot have this violence in my school, Annelise.'

'Violence? Where did I write that the punishment should be violent?'

You continue reading:

[*As Mr Nelson*] 'Section Four-point-one: The aforementioned punishment should be violent—very violent."

'If Ryan Morby can inflict pain on others, he should be prepared for others to do the same in return.'

[*As Mr Nelson*] 'You have no such power, Annelise! You are not Head Girl! You are just a representative of the Chapel choir!'

A gasp.

[*As Mr Nelson*] 'Annelise, I was at Bunnings this morning buying … supplies.'

' … What supplies, sir?'

[*As Mr Nelson*] 'Pesticide. I'm so sorry, Annelise. Let me get you some water.'

You leave the office and I am … alone.

What is happening? Could this be? Is this the end?

A pause.

… No.

I snatch the set of car keys from your desk and leave, passing you by the water cooler:

[*As Mr Nelson*] 'Where are you going, Annelise?'

'Business to attend to, sir. Chapel choir business.'

Twelve twenty-five p.m.: I'm power walking through the Science Building, the tuck shop; opening my locker, I pick my weapon of choice: hockey stick.

The power in the palm of my hand.

There's fifteen minutes before lunch. And before I eat my caprese salad, I've got some walls to smash through.

I begin in the Music building. The students are all in practice rooms so don't hear the sound of splintering plasterboard. When there are enough holes, I wait:

One, two, three … five … ten … twenty …

BE FREE YOU BROWN BANDED BEETLES!

Next, the English building, then Maths, then the gym:

Hundreds, thousands … millions, gathering around my feet, crawling toward the sun.

Finally, covered in white dust and plaster, I am standing next to your car, Mr Nelson, and I am … conflicted.

I considered us equals, once. Colleagues, even … friends. But you disrespected the fabric on which I have built my legacy. And now you must pay.

Twelve fifty p.m.: The bell finally tolls.

Students, teachers and cockroaches alike swarm the corridors as I battle my way through screaming children.

I know where I'll find him. I'm coming.

'Hey, Turd Blossom!'

Ryan turns, his black shoes covered in the remains of my squashed kin:

[*As Ryan*] 'Was this your dumb idea?'

I nod.

'I'm gonna kick your ass, Ryan.'

Ryan gives me one last middle finger as I reach into my blazer pocket for the can of pesticide from your boot and … SPRAY!

He writhes on the ground like the vermin he is:

[*As Ryan*] 'You're a penis, Annelise Ashley!'

'No, Ryan Morby—you're a penis.'

A pause.

Now, Principal Nelson, before you think about calling the police, I will leave with you one final provocation:

The cockroach can survive in almost any environment: jungle, desert, arctic, sea. The cockroach is passionate, generous, loyal and always arrives on time.

But the one environment it truly thrives in is the fascist walls of a totalitarian private school.

You have been blind for far too long, my dear Principal. It's time for a new regime.

ANNELISE *reaches for the petition under her chair.*

Now, would you please sign my petition?

She holds out the pen.

Lights out.

THE END

Forts Until the Crack of Dawn
Caitlin Monk

JACK, *14, male-identifying*

LUCY, *17, female-identifying*

Gender is not key to the performance of this piece, performers are welcome to edit pronouns and character names to their comfort.

In a young teenager's bedroom. There is a bed and a temporary sleeping arrangement; the impermanence and makeshift nature of this can be demonstrated by a sleeping bag, a pillow and blanket, etc., things that are simple, bare and impermanent.

The space should look as if a teenager has been given five minutes to clean their room—clothes in messy piles, gaming consoles, books and toys strewn about the space.

LUCY *sits on the floor with her hands over her face taking deep controlled breaths.* JACK *enters.* LUCY *bolts upright with a full smile.*

LUCY: Oh, hey booger boo!

JACK: I told you not to call me that.

LUCY: Well, there's actually a secret clause in your birth certificate that says as your older sibling, I automatically get the front seat in the car and any and all name-calling privileges.

JACK: Yeah well, I told you to stop, it's embarrassing and stupid. Like you.

LUCY: When did you get so moody?

JACK: When did you start pretending to care?

LUCY: Hey I care!

> *Beat.*

Your room's cool.

> *Beat.*

Sooooo, how have you been?

JACK: Fine.

LUCY: More than a one word answer?

JACK: Piss off.

> LUCY *laughs, and* JACK *relaxes.*

Is Grandma sick?

LUCY: No, just old, and sick of being old.

JACK: So why are you looking after her?

LUCY: I think Mum and Dad just told you that. I have been staying with Grandma but I'm more of a pain than a help.

JACK: So you picked not to be home.

LUCY: Hey I'm here now. What do you want to talk about?

JACK: I don't want to talk to you.

LUCY: Fine.

I'll just talk and talk and talk and you will just have to stay up till the crack of dawn listening to my every thought.

> *She settles herself in, takes a deep breath.*

I think I want to get bangs. I know when you cut me bangs when I was sleeping as revenge for breaking your favourite Beyblade, I hated them but I'm starting to warm up to the idea. I saw Grandma in the nude and we haven't really talked about it. I think I have developed a horrible psychological Pavlov's-dog-type reaction where I fart every time I walk past the counter at work and I don't know if people have noticed. Also I lost my pair of Vans and I didn't realise how much I wore them until they were gone and it's breaking me a bit.

> *She inhales another deep breath.*

JACK: Please no, that was more than enough.

LUCY: How was dinner?

JACK: Awkward. I think they thought you were going to eat with us. They made you a plate and got the cordial you like.

LUCY: Wasn't hungry.

JACK: You could have come down.

LUCY: I'm tired. The drive from Grandma's is so long, plus being here is hard enough. I'm not in the mood for a verbal sparring match at the moment, bud.

JACK: You don't know that would happen.

LUCY: Do you remember when you were little—
JACK: Lucy—
LUCY: You were little and you were afraid the boogeyman was coming to get you at night so we would—
JACK: I don't remember that.
LUCY: You didn't let me finish.
JACK: They just wanted to talk to you.
LUCY: And I'm trying to talk to you.

> JACK *rolls his eyes.*

Anyway … So we would make a blanket fort and share all our fears and secrets so the boogeyman couldn't scare you.
JACK: Get out of my room!
LUCY: Get out of my face.
JACK: How 'bout you go run away again.
LUCY: How 'bout you stop being a baby.
JACK: I'm not being a baby, you just left, you didn't say goodbye, you didn't even tell us where you went or what happened. I'm not a baby, you are just a bad sister. I don't want to talk about stupid forts with the worst person ever.
LUCY: You know … I … you just … you don't know anything. Just go to bed, unless you're still too scared to.

> *Pause.*

JACK: I'm not scared of anything anymore.
LUCY: Yeah right.
JACK: I'm not.
LUCY: Not ghosts?
Not the creepy mum from *Coraline*? Not our mum?
JACK: No. Not Mum. I'm not scared of any mums. The thought of Grandma naked is pretty scary though. You scared of Mum?
LUCY: For sure, all mums are scary. I can outrun Grandma or confuse her with Facebook or even distract her with Millionaire Hot Seat. But mums are biologically hardwired to have all their focus on their children and Mum's wires and mine tend to get crossed pretty easily.
JACK: She looked for you.
When you left she was driving around for two days straight. She called everyone we have ever known.

She cried a lot. Dad has been really quiet since.

LUCY: Yeah I assumed she worked out who I was staying with when Grandma was waiting outside of IGA for me.

[*As Grandma*] 'I'm not gonna force ya back, you will just bolt again, too strong willed. But I can't have my only granddaughter living on the street like an urchin. Now you either come stay with me or you go back to your mum and dad's.'

JACK: You haven't said sorry yet.

LUCY: Pardon?

JACK: To Mum and Dad, you haven't said sorry yet.

LUCY: Yeah well, neither have they.

JACK: You're the one who ran away.

LUCY: They were the ones who told me to leave.

JACK: You weren't actually supposed to.

LUCY: You're too young to get it so stop trying, okay booger boo? Go to sleep.

JACK: Why are you here?

LUCY: Because Mum turned my room into storage the moment I left as if she was counting down the minutes.

JACK: No—Why are you here, why are you back home? Why aren't you at Grandma's?

LUCY: I was in a bit of a rush when I left here, and now I need my birth certificate and my passport to get my licence. I think at the time I thought I'd be back here after a week, not three years.

JACK: I hope you fail the test.

LUCY: I probably will.

JACK: Where—um, where will you go? When you get your licence.

LUCY: Anywhere, as far as I can I guess, might settle down in Byron or something, become a hippie, clear my life of negative energy.

JACK: What, NO!

Beat.

Dad was the one who told Mum to use your room for storage. They had a big fight about it, but Mum just gave up. It wasn't Mum.

LUCY: The who doesn't really matter, booger boo, more that they did it. They don't want me back.

JACK: I do.

There's a silence as they look at each other.

It's not fair.

LUCY: Yeah I know, but we only have to bunk together for one night then I'm out of your hair.

JACK: No. It's not fair that everyone else gets a sister but me.

LUCY: You have a sister. I'm right here, booger boo.

JACK: No you're not. You're only here till you leave tomorrow.

You're here till you get your stuff and go and get your licence and go be a hippie. You're here because you have to be, not because you want to be around me.

You weren't at my soccer final, you weren't at the school play. You weren't here when the basement flooded. You weren't even here for my birthday, or the birthday after that or the one after that. If you're my sister, you're the worst sister in the world.

Everyone else gets to hate their sister. Except me, I sit here and hope you come back. It's not fair, I should hate you and hate you and, you're ugly and annoying and I miss you.

Beat.

LUCY: Oh bud, I'm so sorry.

JACK: No, you're not. If you were sorry you wouldn't be about to do it again. You wouldn't be staying here tonight to go back to Grandma's, you would just be here and stay here.

LUCY: I'm sorry you have a bad sister, booger boo.

JACK *head snaps up with a stern look.*

Sorry, Jack. I'm sorry you have a bad sister, Jack. But I can't stay here, we would all fight too much, too much has gone on. I will drive to you first thing when I get my licence.

Beat.

JACK: And call me?

LUCY: Yes, bud.

JACK: And come to my soccer games?

LUCY: When I can.

JACK: And visit?

LUCY: Maybe you could visit me?

JACK: Okay.

LUCY: Hey Jack?

JACK: Yeah?

LUCY: You have really grown up.

JACK: Yeah, I have a beard now.

LUCY: I thought that was sauce.

JACK: You suck.

They smile at each other.

LUCY: Hey Jack?

JACK: Yep?

LUCY: Do you really think I'm a bad sister?

JACK: No, I'm just mad at you still. Do you really want bangs?

LUCY: Yeah I think so.

JACK: Can I do them?

LUCY: Not a chance, bud.

JACK: Hey Lucy?

LUCY: Yeah?

JACK: Can we make a blanket fort and tell secrets?

LUCY: Do you have any good secrets?

JACK: Yeah. I kissed Maddie while she was dating Tom and she broke up with him for me and I think I like Tom more than her.

LUCY: I'll get some blankets.

JACK: Me too. I'll get the pillows. I don't have school tomorrow.

LUCY: Secrets in the fort until dawn I guess?

JACK: You will say bye when you have to go?

LUCY: Yeah Jack, I'll say goodbye.

Fade to black.

THE END

Splash

Jake Parker

CHRIS, *15 years old, not sporty in the slightest.*

DERMOTT, *15 years old, has great posture.*

The backyard of a suburban property. The fences are high. The lawn is manicured and sparse.

A slash in the dialogue (/) indicates that the next actor should begin their line, overlapping the two actors' dialogue.

A dash in the dialogue (—) indicates that the current actor speaking is cut off by the next actor.

An ellipsis in the dialogue (…) suggests that the current actor should trail off, leaving a pause.

Morning fills the treetops of a suburban backyard. The business of movement has not yet begun.

CHRIS *is standing on the roof of a house wearing Batman pyjamas and a bicycle helmet with googly eyes and pipe cleaners sticking out. His eyes are fixed on something down below.*

DERMOTT *enters by taking a final step onto the roof. He slumps and catches his breath.*

DERMOTT: Is this where you eat your Cheerios these days?
CHRIS: Don't be an idiot.
DERMOTT: Sorry. Of course. I forget that you're a Fruit Loops man.
CHRIS: I'm not even hungry.
DERMOTT: No kidding. Do you know how early it is?
CHRIS: It's six a.m.—
DERMOTT: It's early enough to hear the garbage men take their first leak of the day.

CHRIS: That's exaggerating.

DERMOTT: Well when you invited me over for a *Rick and Morty* marathon, I thought that'd mean we'd have a big Saturday sleep-in. Instead we're planning breakfast on your rooftop.

CHRIS: I didn't ask you to come up here.

DERMOTT: What are you even doing?

CHRIS: I'm … Building myself up to it.

DERMOTT: Up to what?

CHRIS: [*pointing down below*] The pool.

Beat.

DERMOTT: You mean you're gonna … ?

CHRIS: Do an epic cannonball in the pool. Yes.

DERMOTT *peers over the edge and whistles.*

DERMOTT: That's pretty risky man.

CHRIS: I've seen videos on YouTube.

DERMOTT: Okay but—

CHRIS: And almost half of them didn't include the word 'FAIL'.

DERMOTT: I really think—

CHRIS: If I just bend my knees the right way.

DERMOTT: Chris—

CHRIS: And step two metres beyond the edge.

DERMOTT: You'll be / cooked.

CHRIS: I'll be fine … [*Breathes in deeply*] Probably.

DERMOTT: This is messed up, even for you. And you've pulled some crazy ones on me. Remember that time at school when you ate peanut butter with celery for lunch?

CHRIS: People eat that all the time!

DERMOTT: Okay, well, just say '*celery sticks*' when you want me to come rescue you.

CHRIS: I'm not gonna say that.

DERMOTT: *Celery. Sticks.*

CHRIS: You don't get it.

DERMOTT: You're right. I don't. What are you trying to prove here? I mean, you're in your Batman pyjamas, puffing up your chest like you're Darren in PE class—

CHRIS: I'm nothing like him.

DERMOTT: I know you're not. You can at least count without using your fingers.

CHRIS: Exactly.

DERMOTT: Exactly. So let's just go back down before you're remembered as the kid who believed he could fly.

CHRIS: Stop doing that.

DERMOTT: Doing what?

CHRIS: Implying that I'm an idiot.

DERMOTT: I'm / not.

CHRIS: You are.

> *Beat.*

DERMOTT: You're right … I'm sorry. [*In Batman's voice*] You're Batman.

> *They both chuckle. Then a long, awkward silence.* CHRIS *massages his cheeks, unsure of what to do.*

CHRIS: How'd you sleep?

DERMOTT: Fine, fine.

CHRIS: Good … Good.

> *Beat.*

DERMOTT: Crazy dreams but.

CHRIS: Oh yeah?

DERMOTT: We were on the world's most lethal rollercoaster.

CHRIS: The Headspin Roller!

DERMOTT: Yeah. The one that's meant to make you pass out and see purple.

CHRIS: Wicked.

DERMOTT: We were rolling on the track and you looked like you were gonna spew. And when we got to the top, you turned to me and said: 'I'm farting like my mum in a yoga class'.

> DERMOTT *laughs and does a downward dog.* CHRIS *remains silent and takes a step closer to the edge.*

Would you stop edging closer? I'm not gonna call the ambulance if your shin ends up in your shoulder. Ever seen *that* video?

CHRIS: That's not funny.

DERMOTT: Then do it. Do it if you're so brave.

CHRIS: I'm just … finding the right angle.

DERMOTT *walks over to* CHRIS *and flicks the pipe cleaners on his helmet. It's almost like he's doing karate.*

DERMOTT: Come on!

CHRIS: Quit it!

DERMOTT: It's not me, it's a magpie!

He makes a magpie sound.

CHRIS: I mean it, Dermott!

DERMOTT: Alright, alright … [*Looks down*] Ugh! As if you'd want to jump in that festy water. It's a full on insect cemetery.

Beat.

Where's your dad?

CHRIS: What?

DERMOTT: Your dad. Where is he?

CHRIS: I dunno.

DERMOTT: Yeah you do. Look, your knee's doing that wobbly thing when you can't think of an excuse.

CHRIS: [*slapping his knee still*] You've read *one* mastermind book. Stop thinking you can read my mind.

DERMOTT: Fine. But I swear your dad's usually scooping a fly out of that pool the second it makes a ripple.

Beat.

CHRIS: He's inside.

DERMOTT: For real? How have I not seen him?

CHRIS: He just hasn't come out of his room for a while.

DERMOTT: Oh … Is he … On the internet?

CHRIS: No. Gross. Shut up.

DERMOTT: Where's your mum then?

Pause.

Chris?

CHRIS: Do you remember the old jetty? Before it collapsed?

DERMOTT: Yeah, why?

CHRIS: Did you ever used to, like, jump off it?

DERMOTT: Always. I'd do backflips there with the guys. We had to stop when Darren messed one up and lost all of his teeth but.

CHRIS: Oh.

DERMOTT: That was all before we started hanging out. You know I never really liked them. When they bullied you and all that.

CHRIS: Yeah … I know.

> *Beat.*

Anyway I could never do it. Jump, I mean.

DERMOTT: Because you saw Darren swimming around for his teeth?

CHRIS: No. I dunno. There were kids younger than me who'd sprint down. They'd make a splash arse-first into the darkest part of the water. But I just … clung to the railing.

DERMOTT: Okay, now you're fully turning into a Tim Winton novel.

CHRIS: Aw, whatever.

DERMOTT: No, come on. What were you so afraid of?

> *Pause.*

CHRIS: Stingrays.

> *Beat.*

They look like human faces that have been sliced off and rolled out like pizza dough. I can't deal with the idea of, like …

DERMOTT: What?

CHRIS: One, like, smiling at me.

> *Beat.*

DERMOTT: Like this?

> DERMOTT *pulls his mouth wide and imitates a stingray smile.*

CHRIS: [*unamused*] At some point Mum just started diving in without me. I'd sit on the edge of the jetty and hold her ice cream. But it'd always melt down my fingers by the time she got back. That ever happen to you?

DERMOTT: Sticky ice-cream fingers? Sure.

CHRIS: Not that.

DERMOTT: Oh. I dunno. Mum and Dad were kinda cheesy. They'd always insist we hold hands and jump in together.

CHRIS: Oh.

DERMOTT: I guess I wasn't, like, hard work as a kid or whatever.

CHRIS: What's that supposed to mean?

DERMOTT: Well … You're not really like everybody else at school.

CHRIS: So?

DERMOTT: So sometimes it seems like you had a hard upbringing or something. Like, we have this book at home that says kids with attachment issues have a tendency to, y'know, act out.

> CHRIS *is silent.*

It means you seek attention!

CHRIS: I can't believe you!

DERMOTT: Look at what you're doing! You're only proving me right.

CHRIS: I'm *this* close to pushing you over the gutters.

DERMOTT: Ah come on. Don't be a sicko.

CHRIS: I bet you'd like that, anyway. Teenage hero saves bullied loser from just another stupid teenage stunt. You take every chance you can get to be the saviour of the story. News flash, Dermott. You're just an annoying kid who's always trying to sit at the adult's table. The real question is, who are *you* trying to impress?

DERMOTT: You're such a dog.

CHRIS: And so are you. The difference is you can't chew a real bone.

DERMOTT: Then who's Johann?

CHRIS: What?

DERMOTT: Johann. You kept saying that name in your sleep last night.

CHRIS: No I didn't.

DERMOTT: Pathetic!

CHRIS: He's nobody. He's a hacky sack nobody!

DERMOTT: As if.

CHRIS: Please, just stop.

DERMOTT: Where's your mum, Chris?

> CHRIS *shoots a look at* DERMOTT *like he might vomit or scream.*

CHRIS: Please, Derm.

DERMOTT: Come on, say it. She's gone.

CHRIS: Celery sticks.

DERMOTT: She finally had enough of your weirdo outbursts.

CHRIS: Celery sticks!

DERMOTT: Taken the family car and motored off to a better life in the city.

CHRIS: CELERY! STICKS!

> CHRIS *tears off the helmet and hugs it with all his might. He kneels into a ball and cries.*

DERMOTT: I'm sorry. I only guessed. I didn't think ... I didn't think.

> DERMOTT *perches himself at arms length from* CHRIS.

When did she leave?

CHRIS: Three days ago. I heard some yelling outside. Went down to see what was happening. But when I opened the door, it was just Dad. Kneeling on the driveway. Staring at an oil stain.

I should have noticed earlier. But it all happened in slow motion. She started buying groceries in bulk. Probably knew Dad would be useless ... And then there were the late-night calls.

DERMOTT: With Johann.

CHRIS: With Johann.

DERMOTT: Tosser sounds like he has a criminally greasy man bun.

> *Pause.*

I'm really sorry, mate. I don't actually think you're a weirdo.

CHRIS: Yeah you do. But it's okay. Thanks for saying that anyway ... [*Wiping eyes*] Blah. Sorry.

DERMOTT: Don't be.

CHRIS: It's so stupid. I thought ... if I could jump, maybe I wouldn't be that wimpy kid anymore. I wouldn't be the reason that she left.

DERMOTT: You couldn't be the reason.

> *Beat.*

You're way too entertaining to leave behind.

CHRIS: [*chuckling*] That's exaggerating.

> *Beat.*

DERMOTT: We should give ourselves some credit. Adults lose their heads *way* more than crazy hormonal kids. We've gotta remember that. We've gotta keep them in check.

CHRIS: You're right.

DERMOTT: Damn straight.

The sound of a car pulling up into the driveway.

CHRIS: Mum?

> CHRIS *half runs, half crawls across the roof as if every glimmer of hope is just offstage. The car door slams. His shoulders drop when he realises it's not her.* DERMOTT *hangs his arm over* CHRIS*'s shoulder.*

DERMOTT: How about a crunchy mug of Fruit Loops?

CHRIS: Yeah. Sounds nice.

> CHRIS *crouches as if he's about to climb down.*

DERMOTT: You're not going down *that* way are you?

> DERMOTT *makes suggestive eyes at the pool.*

What do you say?

CHRIS: [*smiling*] I say you're crazy.

The two friends stand side by side.

DERMOTT: Three.

CHRIS: Two.

DERMOTT *and* CHRIS*:* ONE!

> *They howl like wolves and jump. The lights go down before the sound of a splash baptises the day.*

THE END

I Really Like You
(*Or; Pen, Paper, Subway Cookies, Legal Studies and Everything That Conspired for Us to Find Each Other*)
Pip

A, *14–17, human being—a very scholastic person; is nervous at parties, loves small, random acts of kindness.*

B, *14–17, human being—does not vibe with classes; loves a bevvie, footy and anything that makes them feel great.*

Setting: There is none. Just two people. Commonplace objects (chairs, stools, drama blocks, etc.) may be used to help the actor feel anchored in the space, but try and keep away from characterising individual scenes with sets/props.

Time: Time moves at a breakneck speed through this play. A time jump is indicated by a double paragraph space, but these are not pauses (they are for the Actor's use only). The theatrical challenge is to present the time jumps while maintaining the feeling of a single conversation—try to find other ways to bring clarity to the story telling.

Pauses: Actors are allowed to add one pause each at their discretion, not including the single notated 'beat'. Otherwise, pace should be snappy with breaks non-existent.

An overlap occurs when a / is written; the next character's line should begin where this symbol appears.

... indicates a trailing off.

— indicates being cut off either by themselves or by the other character.

Words or lines in brackets ( ) indicate what a character would have said if they weren't cut off. These are not to be said out loud.

A: Your pen.

B: Huh?

A: Your pen.

B: It's in my (pocket)—

A: Nope—it's right here, in my hand. Here ya go.

B: Um …

A: Thanks?

B: Yeah.

A: No worries.

B: It's really loud in here huh!

A: Huh?

B: Do you wanna drink? There's—

A: What!?

B: You look super cool!

A: I look like a fool!?

B: Cool! You look really cool!

A: Oh—I have a / boyfriend!

B: I know! Bill's a mate! Just saying you loo(k) … Usually you say thanks?

A: Why are you talking to me?

B: I just said you look cool! Take a chill pill, will ya?

A: Sh.

B: I'm building my social circle, it's an im/portant part of high school …

A: Your social circle doesn't need to affect my algebra test.

B: Stop being such a teacher's pet, will you?

A: I'll stop being a pet when you stop being a jerk.

B: There's more to life than just school, is / all I'm saying.

A: Not when you're in class. Why do you even come?

B: Because I have to?

A: Because—

    What if you wanted to be here?

B: I don't.

A: Then what do you want? Do you *want* just footy with the boys? Wagging to get a cookie from Subway? Is that all?

B: I dunno.

A: Y'do. Just (try)—

B: Just back off, what about that?

How do you know about the Subway cookies?

A: Excuse me?

B: Sorry for yelling at you the other day.

A: You didn't have to wait the whole weekend y'know—could've apologised that afternoon.

B: 'That's okay.'

A: Huh?

B: 'That's okay.' 'It's all good.' 'Thanks for apologising.'

A: Just yelling at someone isn't all good. It was embarrassing.

B: You *were* being pushy but—

A: Is this a real apology?

B: Yes.

A: I forgive you then.

B: Do you mind if I borrow some paper?

A: As long as you give it back.

B: Oh—I'm gonna write on it … actually. So … I mean I can / if you want—

A: I'm joking, it's fine.

B: Hey, I bought you this double chocolate chip … to say thanks for the paper.

A: You didn't have to do that.

B: Nah, that was solid lending me that. Lost my backpack on the bus, like an idiot.

     Are you okay?

A: Yeah, I'm fine … Just um—Bill and I kissed—he's been (weird)—God! Why'd I get a boyfriend?

     Are you okay?

B: What—huh—yeah.

A: I'm sorry about that … he punched you really hard.

B: I'm okay.

A: You're bleeding.

B: I'm okay.
A: Are you doing much over the holidays?
B: Dad gets boozed up at Chrissy but that's 'bout it.
A: What do *you* do though?
B: Play video games … watch movies—What are you, my mum?
A: I'm just interested in what you like. That's what friends do, right?
B: Friends?
A: Yeah like—are (we friends?)—Like I also like movies for example. *Abigail's Party* is my favourite.
B: Yeah? You're gonna do Film next year?
A: If it runs, it's at the top of my list.
B: Well fingers crossed.

    Did you get the elective you wanted?
A: Third backup … Legal Studies. Film didn't run.
B: Dang.
A: What'd you get?
B: First choice.
A: PE?
B: Legal Studies.
A: Plot twist.
B: What?
A: I seem to recall 'I just don't want to be in class' being something you said?
B: I just don't like maths. Anyway you're the one who told me to figure out what I did want. And this is it.

A: So we should study together, we'd complement each other well, I think. Where do you sit at lunch?
B: You know.
A: I don't.
B: You do.
A: Shut up. Just—give me your phone.
B: What? No.
A: I don't care about your porn stash, I'm just giving you my Insta.
B: Don't have Insta.
A: Oh … Really?

B: Don't really get it. Hey, I'm not really interested in dating / anyone right—

A: It's not a date! It's not. It's study.

B: Understood. Sorry.

A: Do you have Facebook?

B: I'm not fifty.

A: What do you have?

B: A phone.

A: Are you one of those people who / wear khakis and sandals and stay off the grid?

B: Do I think I'm better than everyone? 'Cause I don't have—No. No I'm just, like, eighty and can't be bothered with all that.

A: Nah, I think it's fully sick hey.

B: Are you trying to talk like me?

A: What? No. No! No …

B: You don't—you don't / have to—

A: I wasn't!

B: I can understand you fine.

A: Maybe I'm just not as vanilla as you think.

B: Oh yeah?

A: Oh yeah. I'm with it.

B: Jesus Christ.

A: Oh—

B: Sorry. Are your parents home?

A: Heard them come in a few minutes ago. It's not like they're super intense about that stuff just … My dad works in a library, I'm basically a walking wool cardigan.
    I wasn't trying to copy—I hope I didn't offend you.

B: Nah it's funny! Like weird, but funny weird y'know?

A: Like not having Insta?

B: Why not.

A: Anyway, *Abigail's Party* is a damn masterpiece of cinema and no-one can tell me otherwise!

B: I—no joke—I have never, ever heard of it.

A: It's just like … funny and witty and clever.

B: What's it about?

A: This couple are hosting a dinner party with this woman who lives in their … tenement? Neighbourhood? Anyway, her daughter's having a party and they're trying to suck up to the upper—

B: So wait who's Abigail?

A: The lady's daughter.

B: So then—

A: It's not about Abigail.

B: But—

A: It's the inciting incident.

B: The what?

A: No way.

B: I'm not a nerd like you.

A: I'm not a nerd!

B: Sure.

A: We should get back to study—So it's like Nadia's.

B: Nadia's?

A: That big house party where the police got called? All those Year Sevens were caught TPing the neighbour's house? Come on, everyone was at that.

B: Yeah but … Ragers like *that*—not usually my speed.

A: But you're at parties all the time.

B: Yeah 'cause my mates are.

A: You just show up?

B: Aw … Nah I get invited, but like … I mean, last Wednesday I went to that beach gatho 'cause Tom wanted to pash a chick there and I said I'd wingman for him. Can I scab two dollars for a sausage roll?

A: Sure. And did you? Wingman?

B: Yeah—I'm like the best wingman. Anyway—you were at Nadia's, you gonna tell me you don't like a party?

A: I was only there 'cause of Bill.

B: See? You're going to parties to pash people, I'm going to help people pash, it's the same thing.

A: That was one party. You're at one every week.

B: But—

A: Do you drink?

B: Aw … yeah but like not so much now. Getting a bit old for bingeing I reckon.

A: I—Okay.

B: What?

A: How much do you drink, to be needing to stop at our age? Like you're (an alcoholic)—
    I have to go—

B: I feel like you're judging me for the drinking thing.

A: Why would I—can we do this after class?

B: I don't care (about class).

A: Why would I judge you for that? Not like you're the only one …

B: You could be judging everyone.

A: Then why would you care?

B: 'Cause I'm part of everyone.
    I just—I don't have a problem!

A: That what your dad says at Chrissy?

    Hey, have you been getting my texts?

B: Yeah.

A: Okay … So …
    Why are you ignoring me?

B: Busy.

A: Look I'm sorry I said that about your—

    What's going on? I'm sick of the silent treatment.
    Did you drop Legal Studies?

B: If you don't wanna be there, don't come. You told me that.

A: When?

    Are you drunk at school?

B: Will you leave me alone?

A: Come on what are you doing—

    What happened?

B: It's you …

A: It's me. What happened?

B: Alcohol poisoning.

A: Jesus Christ.

B: I'm an idiot.

A: That's nothing new. I bought you raspberry cheesecake.

B: Raspberry—!

A: Best of the Subway cookies.

B: My stomach still hurts from the pump.

A: Ah … right. Okay.

B: Dad's flipped out—hypocrite.

A: Do you—do you need a place?

B: Maybe … far out …

A: You could stay at mine.

B: You—

    Did you break up with Bill?

A: Wha—Yeah, like two years ago …

B: I mean—I heard *he* broke up with *you*.

A: Ah yeah … probably heard that from him.

B: Why'd you do it?

A: Well … we went on a break because the first time we kissed, he spat on the floor straight after.

B: Aw …

A: And we stayed broken up because … he punched you.

B: What?

A: You don't remember?

B: No—I remember … what, did you have a crush on me or something?

A: Yeah that's really funny.

B: I'm full of laughs apparently.

A: Why is the first time we're speaking this year in a hospital?

B: Because I'm dumb.

A: I know what I said about your dad was wrong. I'm sorry.

B: Made me feel like I had a problem …

A: [*a joke*] You're not doing yourself any favours.

B: I know, I'm stupid.

A: Okay stop that now. You're not stupid.

    Is that how I made you feel? Stupid?

B: A bit.

A: I'm sorry.

    Y'know how many people told me *I* was an idiot for hanging out with you?

B: Yeah?

A: Then when you stopped talking to me and I got all upset, it was all 'I told you so'.

B: You got upset?

A: Of course I did! You're like my— (what do we call this?)

B: I didn't give the best first impression.

A: What do you mean?

B: When I called you cool, at Nadia's party. I was a bit of a creepo.

A: At Nadia's?

B: All the toilet paper.

A: That's not where we met, you doofus.

B: Huh?

A: You dropped your pen in the first week of Year Eight. That's where we met.

B: Oh yeah! Year Eight sucked. I finally watched that movie.

A: *Abigail's Party*?

B: It was boring.

A: Honestly, I don't know if it's my favourite anymore anyway.

B: Why?

A: Has a very bleak outlook on class relationships. I figure if I want to stay hopeful about—Well, I don't think it's all that bleak in real life.
     Do you think you'll stop now?

B: Drinking?

A: Yeah.

B: I dunno, maybe.

A: I don't wanna be a spoilsport just … Want you to be safe.

     Beat.

B: Hey …

A: Hey …

B: If I was honest … I'd say I really like you.

A: If I was honest I'd say … me too.

B: You're a pretty honest person.

A: Are you?

B: I'm trying to be.

THE END

Bin Day

Megan Rundle

LAUREN, *14. The leader of the Sustainability Club. Intelligent, determined, and sometimes annoying. Wants to make a difference but doesn't know how.*

CONNIE, *14. The class clown. Quick, rebellious and fearless. Isn't part of the Sustainability Club but will do anything for attention.*

JACK, *14. The sweetheart bestie. Sensitive, logical and gentle. Wants the best for the Sustainability Club.*

SCAB, *14. The mystery. Quiet, secretive and smooth. They're new here, trust them, they know what they're doing.*

The majority of the play is set in the back of a recycling truck; in the spirit of recycling, please use what you have to create the set. Cardboard boxes, plastic bottles, milk crates and anything you'd throw in your recycling bin will work perfectly to create the inside of the truck. These boxes can also be used for seats in Scenes Two and Three.

All characters can be any gender, feel free to change names and pronouns to suit your cast.

The sound of a truck is heard. Lights up. We're in the back of a moving recycling truck. CONNIE, LAUREN, *and* JACK *are standing.* SCAB *is at the back of the truck, looking through recycling. They wait in silence until—*

CONNIE: Lauren?

LAUREN: Yeah, Connie?

CONNIE: Remember when you asked me if I wanted to be in a high-speed heist that was going to turn the school on its head and make me an online sensation?

LAUREN: Yeah?

CONNIE: I didn't think that meant stealing a *rubbish* truck at the bumcrack of dawn, travelling at one kilometre per hour in actual rubbish that smells like Jack's farts.

JACK: I didn't!

LAUREN: Firstly, it's a recycling truck not a rubbish truck. Secondly, this will turn the school on its head, and we need your expertise to do that. You've pulled the most pranks out of any Year Nine in the history of this school, maybe even the world.

CONNIE: Thank you.

LAUREN: [*excitedly*] This is going to be epic. We're gonna park this thing on the oval.

CONNIE: [*sarcastically*] My favourite part of any heist movie! The part where they steal a car and *park* it.

LAUREN: [*chanting*] We have the agility, the civility, the humility because we are the—

JACK *joins in.*

LAUREN *and* JACK: S-U-S-T-A-I-N ABILITY

Beat.

Club!

Beat.

CONNIE: I think you three might have to have a little rethink of that song. But firstly, can we all admit it really stinks in here?

JACK: We're in the back of a recycling truck, what do you expect?

CONNIE: Yeah thanks for mansplaining thickhead, but isn't this place meant to be filled with like cardboard and paper?

SCAB: It's this.

SCAB *throws out a Domino's box to* LAUREN. LAUREN, CONNIE *and* JACK *squat over and open it. An entire pizza is in the box.*

LAUREN: Really? A full pizza? I mean I'd understand a couple crumbs, but this is the full eight slices. You can't recycle food!

CONNIE: Supreme, yes!

CONNIE *takes a slice and starts eating.*

LAUREN: Disgusting.

SCAB: I wouldn't eat that.

CONNIE: [*mouth full*] Huh?

SCAB: I shook the cockroaches off before I threw it.

> CONNIE *starts to gag.* JACK *takes the pizza box away.*

CONNIE: Who the hell is that guy?

LAUREN: Scab. He's new. He joined the Sustainability Club last week and now he's our friend. Don't worry, he's cool.

> SCAB *puts two bottle lids over his eyes.*

CONNIE: Clearly.

LAUREN: Now, is everyone across what happens when we get to school?

ALL: Yep.

LAUREN: Great. I'll tell you again.

ALL: Urgh.

LAUREN: So Connie's brother is currently driving the truck; when we get to school, he'll park it on the oval. We'll get a super cool pic of us with the recycling truck that proves that the Sustainability Club is a club that must be taken seriously. Then we'll get back in and return the truck to the driver.

CONNIE: Yeah, about my brother, we're still good to pay him the hundred bucks yeah?

LAUREN: He said he'd drive if we bought him a sausage roll from the canteen!

CONNIE: He did? Might want to talk to him about that.

JACK: Do you think the truck driver's okay? Like we kinda just left him on the street.

LAUREN: We're just borrowing the truck. I told him that in the letter I left him. He's gonna be fine.

CONNIE: He looked pretty old, Lauren. He might like trip on something and need a hip replacement.

JACK: What!? Guys, this isn't me. I like Conan Gray, I like cross stitching, I like *Sims 2*. I don't like breaking people's hips just to steal a flipping recycling truck.

LAUREN: Jack, what we're doing … It's like the coolest thing anyone has ever done ever.

CONNIE: Hmm I'd dispute that.

JACK: I had to wake up at five a.m. for this. I told my mum I was going for a run. Do I look like someone that goes for runs? She's going to kill me if she finds out I lied to her.

CONNIE: Not at all.

JACK: You don't know my mum.

CONNIE: No I mean you don't look like you go on runs at all.

JACK: Great.

LAUREN: Don't listen to her. Connie, you're meant to be helping us not bullying us.

CONNIE: Bullying? If anything, it's a compliment. I hate runners. I really hate runners.

SPEED BUMP. Recycling goes everywhere.

The hell was that?

JACK: Was it a dead body? We ran over a dead body, didn't we?

SCAB: It's a speed bump, idiot.

CONNIE: As I said before, Jack has a very thick head.

LAUREN: Connie, stop! That's bullying and I won't be a bystander.

CONNIE: Sorry, I didn't realise this was the Sustainability and *Loser* Club.

LAUREN: If you hate our club so much then why did you come?

CONNIE: Because I felt sorry for you, plus you said there would be a heist and I love the movie *Ocean's Eight*. And what Sanda Bullock taught me is that if you really want people to notice you, you gotta do something big. You gotta blow something up. Like when I put tuna in the aircon vent at school and the place stunk of fish for two weeks.

LAUREN: We *are* doing something big. It's big, yet respectful.

CONNIE: The respectful activist, you should put that in your Insta bio. But sure, we won't blow anything up. Whatever you say, boss.

JACK: Blowing things up is actually really bad for the environment. So …

CONNIE: I meant figuratively, not literally.

JACK *gives* CONNIE *a look.*

I listen in English, okay.

JACK: I didn't say anything!

CONNIE: Yeah but you thinked it—thought it. I said thought it.

SCAB: Dumbhead.

JACK *giggles.*

CONNIE: Shut up Scab!

CONNIE *gets a call.*

What the—It's Jordan.

She picks up.

Yo bro, how's that windscreen looking? … What? You're joking.

LAUREN: What is it? What is it?

CONNIE: [*to* LAUREN] It's fine, it's fine, it's just the police.

LAUREN: WHAT.

JACK: My mum is going to KILL ME.

LAUREN *and* JACK *start freaking out.*

CONNIE: Can you two shut the hell up. The police are just parked on the street. They're not on to us. [*To phone*] Jordan, just drive very slowly and—

LAUREN *steals the phone.*

LAUREN: Jordan, it's me, Lauren. Firstly, you said a sausage roll was fine—

CONNIE: Don't lead with that!

LAUREN: Secondly, you need to use this rubbish truck for what it was made for.

CONNIE: Recycling.

LAUREN: Shut up! Well, yes, actually. If we wanna look like a recycling truck, we gotta start picking up some recycling bins. Park the truck at the nearest bin, remember, yellow lid. Use the mechanism next to the wheel to lift the bin and empty it into the truck. You got that?

CONNIE: Also try not to look seventeen.

LAUREN: That too. We need to look like an average recycling truck just doing its thing. Sustainability Club, brace yourselves … We're about to be hit with a whole lot of recycling.

The truck parks. The gang look up, the bin is about to empty on to them. They brace themselves. Blackout.

(*If blackouts aren't possible, have someone throw a soft prop book from side of stage.*)

JACK: Ouch!

Lights up. The truck starts driving. JACK *is on the ground, holding his forehead.*

LAUREN: Jack! Are you okay?

JACK: No!

CONNIE *picks up the book* Twilight.

CONNIE: Ah, the first *Twilight*. Now is this rubbish or recycling? I never know these days.

LAUREN: One book in that whole bin? They could have at least donated it.

SCAB *takes the book off* CONNIE.

SCAB: Trash.

CONNIE *is shocked, she loves* Twilight. LAUREN *goes back to the phone.*

LAUREN: Jordan, have the police moved? … No?

The group cheer.

Keep driving Jordan, we gotta do all the houses now.

CONNIE: You know maybe we shouldn't call Jordan because—

Police sirens start.

It's illegal to drive and be on your phone.

The truck parks.

LAUREN: [*into the phone*] Jordan? Jordan? JORDAN?!

CONNIE: He must have done a runner.

LAUREN: What?

CONNIE: Yeah, you know how I said I didn't like runners before? This is why.

JACK: What do we do!?

CONNIE: Um where's Scab going?

SCAB *is about to exit the truck.*

LAUREN: SCAB.

SCAB: I've always wanted to be Baby Driver.

LAUREN: Scab, no!

CONNIE: Let that man have a dream, Lauren.

LAUREN: Well, we're coming with you.

LAUREN *follows* SCAB, *over the recycling.*

JACK: I guess I can say goodbye to my mother and my *Sims 2* families.

CONNIE: Oh, come on.

CONNIE *takes* JACK *by the hand and they follow the other two. Lights down.*

(*If blackouts aren't possible, the audience can follow the four as they mime getting out the back of the truck and stepping into the front seats of the truck.*)

Lights up. We're at the front of the truck. SCAB *is in the driver's seat. The other three are seated next to him.*

LAUREN: The police must be chasing Jordan, let's go while they're distracted.

JACK: Lauren, it's not too late to back out. The Sustainability Club doesn't need a criminal record.

LAUREN: Sometimes to change the world, you gotta break laws.

CONNIE: That's what I'm talking about! We've got the next Greta Gerwig in our midst!

SCAB: You ready?

SCAB *releases the handbrake.*

JACK: It's Thunberg.

CONNIE: What did you call me?

SCAB: Let's go!

SCAB *presses his foot on the accelerator. Car chase music starts. The gang mimic turning corners, it's silly. The music volume fades down.*

CONNIE: Scab, I never asked you. Why are you called Scab?

SCAB: Had a real bad scab once.

CONNIE: Yeah right, checks out.

The music volume fades back up. They do the silly car things again. Music fades down.

LAUREN: You know, I'm not too sure why we're so serious, we're not being chased by anyone. The police aren't behind us.

JACK: Yeah I was thinking that.

CONNIE: Maybe we be less serious?

Happy fun music starts playing. They smile and bob to the rhythm of the music. But suddenly, police sirens and lights.

SCAB: Bugger.

Car chase music begins again.

JACK: TURN AROUND AND DROP ME HOME.

LAUREN: JACK NO, WE'RE A BLOCK AWAY FROM SCHOOL.

CONNIE: I LOVE THIS SONG.

JACK: WE'RE GONNA GO TO JAIL, LAUREN.

CONNIE: NO SERIOUSLY SHAZAM THIS.

LAUREN: SCAB KEEP DRIVING.

CONNIE: DO YOU KNOW THE WAY?

LAUREN: THE OVAL, SCAB.

SCAB: THIS *IS* THE OVAL.

JACK: THAT'S THE PRINCIPAL'S OFFICE.

SCAB turns the wheel around.

CONNIE: Phew!

JACK: NO, NOT THE PRINT ROOM!

CONNIE: ANYTHING BUT THE PRINT ROOM!

LAUREN: SCAB, KEEP GOING.

CONNIE: WHAT?

LAUREN takes the wheel.

LAUREN: TO BE NOTICED YOU GOTTA GO BIG.

ALL: AHHHHHHHHHHHHHHHHH!

Lights down. Lights up. The four of them are sitting on different boxes outside the principal's office. They all look destroyed.

JACK: You okay Lauren?

CONNIE: Hey, at least we didn't hit the office. I'm sure the Principal is about to thank us for not destroying her place of work.

LAUREN: Yep.

JACK: Would have helped if Scab knew where he was going.

SCAB: I've been at this school a week.

CONNIE: And no-one was hurt!

LAUREN: I destroyed a building Connie. Paper went flying everywhere.

CONNIE: It's not our fault the print room is a crappy demountable next to the oval.

LAUREN: We're going to be the laughing stock of the school.

JACK: I'm gonna text my mum. Give her some time to pack my bags to send off to military academy. Soz Mum.

JACK gets out his phone.

CONNIE: Do they even have military academy in Australia?

SCAB: They don't.

CONNIE: How would you know?

SCAB: I know a lot about the military.

JACK: Guys.

CONNIE: You're a mysterious guy Scab.

JACK: Guys.

CONNIE: I'd love to see a photo of that scab one day—

JACK: GUYS. Check your phones.

They each get their phones out.

LAUREN: Holy—

CONNIE: Cow.

LAUREN: We're—

CONNIE: FAMOUS.

The gang read the headlines.

'The Sustainability Club at Dorkell High have cleverly crashed a recycling truck into the print room, proving the overuse of paper in Australian schools.'

JACK: 'A genius print room crash demonstrates that schools need to go digital.'

SCAB: 'The school was going to knock down that demountable anyway.'

LAUREN: My email is flooded guys. Email after email, students wanting to join the club. This one says …

She reads.

'That amount of paper is insane, how do we sign up?' Another says, 'I want to help save the world.' Oh, oh and this one, 'I love your work, let's destroy more school property … ' Okay maybe not that one.

CONNIE: Look, now that we're famous, I should be honest. I know I said I felt sorry for you guys before but really, I was just jealous.

LAUREN: Jealous of us?

CONNIE: Well your club just seemed like a bunch of friends hanging out and until now I've never really had that.

LAUREN: Oh you think 'cause you destroyed a building with us means that we're besties?

CONNIE: [*flustered*] Oh um I just, sorry, I thought—

LAUREN: I'm joking! Of course we're friends, you weirdo.

JACK: Come on, bring in that thick head of yours.

The four of them group hug.

LAUREN: Whatever happens after this, the Sustainability Club lives on.

CONNIE: We're legends!

The group cheers.

THE END

The Bell Tolls

el waddingham

PARIS, *quiet but biting, fiercely intelligent but also deeply shy. First speaker.*

ELLIOT, *creative and sensitive, a pretentious artist in the making. Second speaker.*

DONNA, *outspoken and hardworking, will be Prime Minister in thirty years. Third speaker.*

RUBY, *popular and well-meaning, a bit of a dropkick. Forced into debating for extra marks in English. Timekeeper.*

Setting: A Catholic high school English classroom. Four plastic school desks and chairs stand in a line across the stage. They're coated with a thick layer of notepaper, index cards, pens, McDonald's Frozen Cokes, pencils and highlighters, imbued with a sense of academic terror. Oh— it's summer too. Summer in Northern NSW. Sundrenched and sweaty.

The characters are written as young women but can be played by any actor of any gender identity. Feel free to change pronouns as fit for the cast.

There are a couple of terms throughout that are specific to Queensland (where I went to school, go Maroons) such as 'tuckshop' and 'PTA'. Feel free to alter these terms to align with commonly used language wherever you are from.

These girls are gross, riotous and punky, so just have fun. Be silly. Be emotional and melodramatic. Be all of the things girls are told they shouldn't be.

A classroom. Four girls. An ominous feeling that we've entered a space filled to the brim with bottled chaos and anxiety. DONNA *paces around the room.* RUBY *is staring, absent-minded, at a clock.* PARIS *is writing on and ripping up paper, and* ELLIOT *is dancing in a corner.*

RUBY: Five minutes.

DONNA, PARIS *and* ELLIOT: WHAT?

RUBY: Chill. Don't shoot me. Just the messenger of the fact that you're all about to lose this debate. Again.

DONNA: WE are, Ruby. You're aboard this sinking ship too.

PARIS: My mum is fully going to kill me.

DONNA: If we don't win this case I swear to Gillard, your heads will roll. We cannot lose four rounds in a row, people.

ELLIOT: Mr Hegarty is adjudicating this round, there's no chance he'll let us win over his precious boys.

PARIS: His eyes are like shark eyes and he makes me sweaty and—

RUBY: Four and a half.

ELLIOT: Why'd you join the team if you were just gonna moan about time?

RUBY: I'm the timekeeper. It's my job, duh. Plus, my mum forced me.

PARIS: Same! After the sausage roll incident she told me it was time to 'come out of my shell'—

RUBY: Sausage roll incident?

DONNA: Don't start.

RUBY: Okay … well. Hegarty told my mum I need a couple of extra marks to pass English. It was this or Scrabble club.

PARIS: I have learned to respect old Heggers and his stringent adoration of tradition during my time here, but this topic …

DONNA: 'Men and women are equal at Rainbow Coast Catholic College'. Christ on a cracker.

RUBY: Four minutes.

PARIS: All I have written on my palm card is 'Good evening chairman, ladies and gentlemen'.

ELLIOT: That phrase. It bugs me. We should come up with something less … binary. Like: 'Good day, fellow debating nerds, bored parents and kids with mullets'.

PARIS: True! Breaking down barriers, Elliot. You're revolutionary.

ELLIOT: [*blushing*] I try. I just wish we could start to do things our way.

PARIS: Me too.

DONNA: Yes, yes. Peace and love and whatever, but forget the formalities, Elliot. Focus on the topic.

ELLIOT: Doesn't stuff like that bother you? All the formalities make me feel like a robot. Some old dude decided that in order for young people to be taken seriously, we have to follow these tyrannical rules to form a polite, well-reasoned argument. Where's the burning passion, the emotion? Who am I in a sea of other little girls in uniforms spouting 'good evening chairman, ladies and gentlemen'?

RUBY: [*suddenly full of beans*] Uniforms! One of our arguments could be about uniforms—

ELLIOT: Go, Ruby!

RUBY: —and how there are totally double standards for our uniforms. I can't count the number of times Mr Hegarty's told me to unroll my skirt because it's 'too provocative' above my knees while the boys go around in those stupid tiny AFL shorts. There isn't even a girls' AFL team! How unfair … right, ladies?

DONNA: No, Ruby …

PARIS: We are affirmative. That is an argument for negative.

RUBY: Awh, sorry.

PARIS: True though. My knees aren't 'provocative', they look like smushed cat faces.

ELLIOT: Nah, you've got cute knees.

PARIS: Meow!—

RUBY: Three minutes.

PARIS*'s 'meow' turns into a subdued yelp.*

DONNA: Oh! Oh! YES! I think I have something.

DONNA *continues like she's a cheesy infomercial actor selling the school.*

What if we argued that the school is equal for boys and girls because anyone can win a place here through our extensive scholarship program? The intake of female students has increased because we can use our talent, not wallets, to get where we want.

ELLIOT *and* DONNA *high-five.*

ELLIOT: Equalising the playing field for gifted kids of all backgrounds and genders and diversifying the school ecosystem.

> RUBY *snorts.*

RUBY: We can't use the scholarship kids in our argument.
ELLIOT: Why not?
RUBY: They're not really the shining examples you make them out to be.

> *Tension. Something deeper for Donna.*

DONNA: What do you mean by that, Ruby?
RUBY: They're kind of what happens when you let kids who shoplift for sport into a private school. Rainbow Coast is like the most prestigious school in the area, and we should stick to using people who are actually good examples of the school ethos—like you.
PARIS: She's kind of right. Mum blamed them at the last PTA meeting for all the missing chocolate milk stock at the tuckshop.
DONNA: … I'm on a scholarship.

> *Beat.*

RUBY: No you're not. You? Miss Debate Captain? Miss high-tea with the principal? THE Donna Bartley is a scholarship kid?
DONNA: Why is that so surprising?
RUBY: Well … you act like you're above us.
DONNA: I have to.

> *Beat.*

RUBY: You think you're better than us because you can name every member of parliament. You don't need to act like that all the time—
DONNA: Yes I do! Listen to yourself. You have this idea of who I am based on nothing but assumptions. I'm going to be the first woman in my family to go to university. My mum, my aunts, my grandma, they all tell me how proud they are. All the time. I have to maintain above-average marks in all my classes or my mum has to start to pay school fees, which we can't afford. You have no idea the pressure that comes with. I would love to be spending my time bumming it on Rainbow Beach like you do, but I can't because actually I want to make something of my life.
PARIS: Donna …

Moment. A softening.

DONNA: I'm glad you think less of me, Ruby. That makes me want to prove you wrong even more.

ELLIOT: No-one thinks less of you. You're a bloody badass. You're Donna!

RUBY: [*a bit lost for words*] I didn't know all that. I get it now. I could never think up even half of the stuff you say. This whole team, I don't understand anything you do and I think it's epic. What the heck is a rey-bhu-tahl?

PARIS: Rebuttal. Good try, Rubes.

RUBY: Yeah. [*Chuckles*] Whatever. I'm sorry, okay? I really do admire your—

She notices the clock.

Oh my God, we have two minutes left.

ELLIOT *and* PARIS *scream.*

DONNA: Thank you, Ruby, for your impassioned apology, but, for me, focus! 'Men and women are equal at Rainbow Coast Catholic College'. People, think!

RUBY: Okay. Wild idea. You all wish we could do things our way, so let's do things … our way.

ELLIOT: We could form a coven and hex Hegarty so we win.

PARIS: Coven?

ELLIOT: It means a group of witches.

PARIS: Like a nunnery!

ELLIOT: … Yeah. 'Spose so.

PARIS: You know so much stuff, Elliot. Really cool stuff.

ELLIOT: I think you're really cool.

PARIS: Like cool-cool?

ELLIOT: Yeah.

They smile. Their cute moment is interrupted by RUBY.

RUBY: One minute.

DONNA: Aha! The bell!

ELLIOT: What bell?

DONNA: Mr Hegarty's prized possession. The one that sits on his desk during debates, he rings it to get us to keep to time. That's the patriarchy. He doesn't want us to speak too much, so he moves us along with these arbitrary measures of time that do nothing but hinder us on our journey to liberation.

ELLIOT: Damn, Donna, joining the uprising! Nice to have you, comrade.

PARIS: I'm in too. Screw what my mum thinks. I cannot believe those words just came out of my mouth.

ELLIOT: Yes, Paris! Let's show the world and your mum what a crazy cat you really are!

They meow at each other.

DONNA: Tonight, we go out with a bang. Or, shall I say, a ring? I propose: a new set of rules for the Rainbow Coast Debating Association.

ELLIOT: No more adjudicators, no more Opposition team and definitely no more 'good evenings'.

PARIS: We should not have to hide behind palm cards to be heard.

RUBY: Let them hear what we really have to say.

They form a chattering huddle. An explosion outwards. We're in the debate room now. The heat is on, the audience is the elusive chairman, ladies and gentlemen. DONNA *takes the floor. This should start filled with nervousness, and finish vengeful and enraged. Through* DONNA*'s speech,* PARIS *should sneak really conspicuously off-stage and back on again, to steal Mr Hegarty's bell.*

DONNA: Hi. Hello. Howdy. I know what you're thinking. What is Donna doing up here? She's way too quick-witted to be first speaker! You'd be correct. But I have something to say before we begin. We as the affirmative team … didn't prepare an argument. Sorry. We couldn't think of one single point. We spent the half hour bonding over our shared experiences of *inequality.* My team taught me more than this topic ever could.

ELLIOT: Instead of spending time arguing something we all know is a lie, we built our own set of rules. Against the oppressive bureaucracy of the Debating Association and its patriarchal leaders.

PARIS: So, we are doing things our way. Ushering in a new dawn of debating. One where we can fight back against the topic itself, throw tradition out the window and let our passion and rage light the way.

RUBY is struggling to pronounce 'misogyny', looks to DONNA, *and* DONNA *whispers it to her.*

RUBY: Misogyny has ruled this competition for far too long. Do we really want to live in a world where people like Mr Hegarty still make all the rules?

Unseen, Mr Hegarty makes a move towards his bell.

PARIS: Oh, reaching for your precious bell to shut us up, are you?

PARIS *produces his bell from her pocket.*

Ha. I'm sorry sir, but your reign as adjudicator is over.

ELLIOT *pulls a crown made of paper and a ruler that's been whittled down into a sword from the waistband of her skirt. She bestows* DONNA. DONNA *points the sword at Mr Hegarty.*

DONNA: Time's up, old man.

RUBY: You have two options, relinquish your power to us, or feel our wrath.

ELLIOT: Well?

Mr Hegarty goes to speak. He is silenced by PARIS *ringing the bell.*

RUBY: Oh?

PARIS *rings the bell.*

DONNA: What was that?

Ring ring.

ELLIOT: You won't concede? Very well.

RUBY: ATTACK!

A primal roar. A charge forward.

Blackout.

THE END

Playwright biographies

Taylor Fernandez is an emerging writer currently studying her Masters in Dramatic Writing at the National Institute of Dramatic Art (NIDA). She sits on the Board of the University of Adelaide Theatre Guild and was the 2023 President of their Student Society. In 2022, Taylor was awarded the Young Playwrights' Award by the State Theatre Company of South Australia and Flinders University.

Blake Hohenhaus is a playwright, dramaturg, producer and actor. He is the co-founder of theatre collective Lunch Friend, whose debut work *34 Scenes About the Weather* is slated for publication by Playlab. As a playwright, Blake has developed work through ATYP's National Studio, Playlab's Incubator, ATYP's Fresh Ink, La Boite's Assembly and won Queensland Theatre's Young Playwright's Award (with Zoë Hulme-Peake). As an actor, Blake has performed in schools across Queensland with Shake & Stir. He holds a Bachelor of Creative Arts (Acting & Theatre Studies) and is studying his Masters of Theatre (Dramaturgy) at the Victorian College of Arts.

Aliyah Knight is a Sydney-based actor, writer & director living and working on Gadigal land. She is passionate about telling queer and diverse stories, and representing complex and flawed individuals in their work. Aliyah graduated from AFTRS with a Bachelor of Arts in Screen Production in 2024, having specialised in writing, directing and design. Their final film *Consume* is a queer horror short about the intersection of religious trauma and internalised homophobia. In 2023, Aliyah was selected as one of 20 young writers nationwide for ATYP's esteemed National Studio program. As a result, their queer coming-of-age play *Four Legs Good* was commissioned for ATYP's Intersection Festival, to be held at the Rebel Theatre in 2024. She is currently in development for their first full-length play *Snake-face*, a dark-comedy monologue modern day adaptation of the myth of Medusa. Aliyah has worked as a note-taker with

Roadshow Rough Diamond, and is keen to venture deeper into the world of TV. They are currently developing *Blood Rush*, a horror-comedy pilot about a vampire girlband who accidentally turn one of their super-fans.

Bronte Locke (she/her) studied Theatre at Naarm's Victorian College of the Arts, where she wrote her first play (a post-apocalyptic dog tragedy *Good Boy*). She was an artist-in-residence at Arena Theatre Company and a cast member of the 2020 Melbourne University Law Revue, *Everything is Fine*. Originally from Meanjin, Bronte had the privilege of interning at Queensland Theatre for 2022's *Bernhardt/ Hamlet* (dir. Lee Lewis). She is one half of A Small, Strange Company with Isabelle Carney, whose Melbourne Comfest debut, *The Clit Notes* was sold out for the entire festival. Bronte's television credits include *Bad Behaviour,* a Stan Original miniseries.

Callum Mackay Originally from Sydney/Eora Country, Callum Mackay is an award-winning emerging playwright and actor based in Melbourne/Naarm. Since graduating from the Victorian College of the Arts in 2018 (Bachelor of Fine Arts—Acting), Callum has written four plays: *Brittany & The Mannequins* (Fever103 Theatre), *The Book of Daniel* (Sundries Studio), *Waterfowl* (dir. Hayden Tonazzi), and *the last train to madeline* (Fever103 Theatre). As an actor, Callum has performed with Melbourne Shakespeare Company, Anthropocene Play Company, Ebbflow Theatre Co., and Bloomsday Melbourne. Callum is also the co-founder of Sundries Studio and founded Fever103's Play Readings, currently serving as their literary manager.

Caitlin Monk is a young artist working on Tharawal and Eora Nation and living on Dharawal Country. After finding a passion for the dramatic arts through both her schooling and her family, scriptwriting was discovered to be a perfect meeting of a love of storytelling and an immense passion for reading. She studies at the University of Wollongong doing a double degree in a Bachelor of Arts in Western Civilisations and a Bachelor of Creative Arts. The writing process for Caitlin is deeply intertwined with nature; her work aims to centre on major issues, whether political, philosophical or social, championing raw exploration of the complexities of life.

Jake Parker (he/him) is a writer, editor, and dramaturg, currently completing his MFA in Dramatic Writing at NIDA. Working between Naarm and Gadigal land, his stories implicitly grapple with the concept of an Australian identity. With a background in prose writing, Jake enjoys using absurdist perspectives as a catalyst for both comedic and tender stories. His goal is to entertain, empathise, and subvert audience expectations, all whilst rendering ordinary people extraordinary.

Pip has been a playwright since they were 18. They've written two original works (*I Hope It's Not Raining In London* and *Here, There and Everywhere*) as well as three adaptations (*A Doll's House, Ghosts* and *The Seagull*). They also have a background in Directing for theatre (credits include: *The Crucible, All My Sons, Romeo and Juliet* and many more) They are a strong believer in speaking the unspeakable and giving voice to unique queer experiences.

Megan Rundle is a comedy writer and director from Western Australia. Starting out in the independent theatre scene in Perth, Megan developed her unique brand of humour through writing various comedies and musicals. Her most successful show to date, *Time Capsule*, an original musical, won her a Fringe World Award for best music/musical in 2022. With a commerce degree in marketing, Megan noticed a gap in the Australian entertainment industry for film and television comedies targeted at young Australians. This gap motivated Megan to follow her writing dreams and move to Sydney to study her Masters in Writing for Performance at NIDA. She enjoys bringing fun to the mundane, creating light in times we often find dull and doing it in a clever and hilarious way. Megan hopes to enter the Australian screen and theatre industry, to help Australian young people laugh so much they embarrassingly snort.

el waddingham (they/them), is an eclectic performance artist from Yugumbeh country. As a writer, director, actor, choreographer and dancer, they've worked with Queensland Theatre, QPAC, NIDA, The Farm, La Boite, Browns Mart, Critical Path, Australasian Dance Collective and ATYP. They hold a BFA (Acting & Dance) from the Queensland University of Technology, and are the artistic director of theatrePUNK co., an experimental arts collective based in Meanjin/ Brisbane. el tells stories about magic, women and queerness, blending dance and theatre to bend binaries and break convention. Their playwriting credits include: *Lysistrata* (The B!tch Myth), *Homily*, *Medea* (The Witch of Corinth) and *34 Scenes About The Weather* (co-writer).

Mentor biographies

George Kemp is a writer, theatre maker and educator. He is a graduate of Charles Sturt University and has a Masters from Royal Central School of Speech and Drama, London. He has worked for the last fifteen years with leading theatre companies around the world, including Sydney Theatre Company, Steppenwolf Theatre Company in the USA, Makhampom Living Theatre in Thailand, and multiple theatres across London and Sydney. He writes fiction, non fiction and plays. His plays are performed around Australia and internationally. He has had his non-fiction work published by *Audrey Journal* and short stories by *Sweaty City Magazine*. He was selected to be part of The Faber Academy 2023/2024, run by Allen & Unwin, during which he completed his debut novel *Soft Serve*.

Anchuli Felicia King is a playwright, screenwriter and multidisciplinary artist of Thai-Australian descent. King's plays have been produced by the Royal Court Theatre (London), Manhattan Theater Club (New York), Studio Theatre (Washington D.C.), American Shakespeare Center (Staunton), Melbourne Theatre Company (Melbourne), Sydney Theatre Company, National Theatre of Parramatta and Belvoir Theatre (Sydney). As a screenwriter, King has written episodes on *The Sympathizer* (HBO/A24) starring Robert Downey Jr and Sandra Oh, *Mary and George* (AMC/Sky Atlantic) starring Julianne Moore, *The Baby* (HBO/Sky), *The Twelve*, a trial drama for the Foxtel Group and *Deadloch*, an Amazon original series. She is currently a writer and Executive Producer on *Billion Dollar Whale*, a project in development with Westward Productions and SK Global, based on the non-fiction book of the same name.

Lewis Treston is a multi-award-winning playwright from Brisbane/ Meanjin. Produced plays include: *Hot Tub* (Belvoir 25A), *IRL* (La Boîte), *Hubris & Humiliation* (STC), *An Ideal Husband* after Oscar

Wilde (La Boîte), *Meat Eaters* (NIDA), *Follow Me Home* (ATYP), and *Reagan Kelly* (Metro Arts). He is a graduate from QUT, NIDA and UQ.

Dramaturg

Jane FitzGerald is Resident Dramaturg at ATYP, where she oversees the company's writing programs and commissions, and mentors emerging writers and dramaturgs through the Fresh Ink, National Studio and Cultivate programs. She has worked as Dramaturg for the company on numerous productions and plays. In recent years she has also been Dramaturg on plays for Ensemble, Steps and Holes, and Merrigong. For Sydney Theatre Company she has been Literary Manager, Artistic Associate and administrator of the Patrick White Playwrights' Award as well as a dramaturg on new writing and maInstage productions. She has also been a Literary Manager at Ensemble Theatre (shared role). She has worked as a script reader for the Royal Court London, Playwriting Australia, ANPC and Playworks, and has worked extensively as a Mentor with Year 12 students on HSC creative writing projects.

ATYP Learning

ATYP's Education team creates experiences that connect schools across Australia to our theatre company.

Our programs give students unique insights into the theatre-making process through participating in an ATYP education workshop or seeing an ATYP production (either in person or online).

ATYP offers:

Student Workshops—a practical drama experience to build skills with your students to meet curriculum needs or bespoke performance goals.

Theatre Flat-Pack—the support needed to stage your own ATYP production at your school.

The Intersection Festival—your chance to select and present short plays by Australia's leading young adult playwrights which are then published so they can be used by schools around the country for years to come.

ATYP On Demand—ATYP's digital classroom offers a library of ATYP's past productions (filmed in HD) accompanied by resources that take you deeper into the world of each play.

ATYP On Demand Plus—a unique digital education program for primary schools that uses drama and literacy strategies to teach curriculum areas and concepts in the F-6 Australian Curriculum.

Contact ATYP Education for more details on any of our programs at education@atyp.com.au or 9270 2400.

www.ingramcontent.com/pod-product-compliance
Lightning Source LLC
Chambersburg PA
CBHW050019090426
42734CB00021B/3339